TOPOGRAPHY OF ASSAM

TOPOGRAPHY OF ASSAM

By

JOHN McCOSH

PRINTED BY ORDER OF GOVERNMENT

GYAN

Published by

GYAN

Gyan Publishing House
5, Ansari Road
Daryaganj, New Delhi-110002
Phone: 011-47034999, 9811692060
E-mail: books@gyanbooks.com

Distribution Network
gyanbooks.com
India, USA, Canada, UK, Australia, France

ISBN : 978-81-212-6440-2 (PB)
First Published, 1837

2nd Impression 2022

Printed at: Gyan Press, Delhi.

TOPOGRAPHY OF ASSAM
Author: JOHN McCOSH

TOPOGRAPHY

OF

ASSAM,

BY

JOHN Mc'COSH,

PRINTED BY ORDER OF GOVERNMENT.

1837.

ERRATUM.

I have been led into an error in considering the Eastern divisions of Durrung and Nowgong, under the name of Nowdwar, as a separate district and charge under Major White; whereas Nowdwar is the Eastern division of Zillah Durrung, while Zillah Nowgong extends to the River Dhunseri.

J. M'COSH.

CONTENTS

CHAPTER I.

CHAPTER II.

CHAPTER III.

CHAPTER IV.

CHAPTER V.

CHAPTER VI.

CHAPTER VII.

CHAPTER VIII.

CHAPTER IX.

CHAPTER X.

CHAPTER XI.

CHAPTER XII.

To JAMES RANKEN, Esq., M. D.,

Officiating Secretary, Medical Board,

Bengal.

Sir,

In reply to the Circular of the Medical Board, accompanied by a letter from General Casement, C. B., Secretary to the Government of India, calling for Statistical information, I have the honour to forward the Topography of Goalpara and Gohatti, lately under my Medical charge. Having taken a good deal of interest in the Statistics of Assam generally during a residence of more than two years in the country, and devoted many of my leisure hours towards their investigation, I have now much satisfaction in laying the amount of my knowledge of the whole Province before the Medical Board for the consideration of Government.

Where I have been unable to write from personal experience, I have derived my informaation from an extensive series of Manuscripts kindly furnished me by the Commissioner of Assam, Captain Jenkins; amongst which were Manuscripts of Buchanan, the late Mr. Scott, and the latest Statistical Reports returned to the Commissioner by all the different Officers stationed throughout the Districts; besides a valuable Journal written by Captain Jenkins himself, while on Special Survey in Assam. To have assigned to each Officer the credit due to him in its particular place, would have been a task of great labour and often of difficulty; besides it would in a great measure have been supererogatory, as almost all the papers I have consulted, have at one time or another passed in review before Government.

Where information is drawn from so many sources, it is not easy at all times to preserve consistency throughout, or to write entirely free from error. I am not aware of having transgressed either of these bounds, (further than as stated in the Erratum) though it is not improbable that the eye of the critic may find faults. It may be said that I have written a great deal on men and things I have never seen, and of which I had no experience. To a charge of this kind I have only to reply, that I have had access to the private Journals of men of talent, who have, and endeavoured to communicate the result of their experience: it has been to my disadvantage to be so situated; and had I been vested with the privileges of a deputation, and assisted with an establishment fitted for research, and collecting and recording information, I believe I could have produced something better than what I now offer.

Some apology is due for the manner in which the prints are executed. Wishing to put Government to the least expence possible, I drew them on stone myself, and their being my first attempts in Lithography must plead in excuse for their roughness and inaccuracy. I believe they are more expressive of the features of the country than any written description alone.

I have intentionally avoided the use of all technicalities as well as all attempts at abstract science, and have kept in view the object of being useful to the public in general rather than that of scientific research.

Several portions of this paper have already appeared in the India Journal of Medical Science and in the Journal of the Asiatic Society; these I found it necessary to embody in order to render it complete. I have now exhausted my resources; I trust I have left but few things expected from Topography untouched; and shall consider my labour (which has been considerable) well rewarded, if this should meet the approbation of Government.

I have the honour to be,

Sir,

Your most obedient Servant,

J. M'COSH, *Asst. Surgeon,*

Late of Assam.

GENERAL HOSPITAL,
CALCUTTA,
14*th June*, 1837.

CHAPTER I.

1, Boundaries. 2, Face of Country. 3, Aquatic habits of people. 4, Soil. 5, Brahmaputra. 6, Scenery. 7, Navigation. 8, Route to Bengal by water. 9, Routes to Bengal by land. 10, Via Kassya Hills. 11, Via Dyung and Jetinga. 12, Route to Bootan. 13, Route to Thibet. 14, Route to Burma and China via Hoo-koong. 15, Route from Brahmaputra to Irrawaddi via Noa-dihing. 16, Importance of Road towards China.

ASSAM is that extensive tract of country on
either side of the Brahmaputra; stretching on I.
the N. shore from the river Monash opposite
Goalpara, and on the S. from Nughurbera hill,
about 16 miles above Goalpara, to the foot of
the Himayala mountains, close upon the western
boundary of China. On the N. it is bounded by
a cold mountainous country inhabited by Boo- 1.
teas, Akas, Duphlas, Koppachors, Miris, Boundaries.
Abors, and Mishmis; the first being most west-
ward, and the others eastward in succession;
the Kangtis, Bor-Kangtis, Singphos and Muamarias, separate it on the extreme east from
China and Burma; the Munniporis, Nagas,
Mikirs, Cacharis, Kassyas and Garrows from
our possessions in Sylhet on the south; while
it is connected on the west with Bengal, by the
Zillah Goalpara, late N. E. Rungpore. Though
geographically speaking, Assam terminates at
the river Monash, yet the same peculiar country

I. borders the Brahmaputra as far as Jumalpore: has the same climate, and the same change of seasons. Assam may properly be called the valley of the Brahmaputra, navigable branches intersect it in every possible direction, and there is perhaps not a spot of habitated ground so situated, as to be more than a convenient distance from some navigable stream.

The appearance of the country is very different from that of most others in India; being a perfect flat as far as the eye can penetrate, studded with a multitude of little green conical hills, like hay-cocks in a meadow, rising abruptly from the level plains to the height of from two to seven hundred feet. So very singular
2. Face of Country. are the shapes and arrangement of these mountains in miniature, that the imagination could fancy them the remnants of a country that once stood on the same level with their summits; whose obdurate constituents having resisted the torrents of centuries that washed away the more moveable soil into the Indian ocean, were reserved by Providence as places of shelter and retreat from the floods that periodically inundate the land. Assam is not without some extensive ranges of well cultivated land as is to be found in the zillah of Kamroop. Nor is it entirely composed of alluvial flats; there are some districts of primitive soil far above the reach of inundation, and fit for crops of all kinds. Of these high plains, those at Bishnauth, Chardwar, and Chotegah are the most considerable

Yet strange it is, the inhabitants dont avail themselves of this provision of nature, to raise themselves above the reach of the floods, when they might do so without trouble, expence or inconvenience. They will sit still on the low ground till the water encompasses their huts, and drowns the fires upon their hearths, rather than live comfortably on high dry ground; when the inundation has risen too high for them to wade from one house to another, or even to stand upon their own floors, they paddle out of their houses in canoes, or roost on scaffolds high as the thatch itself, with the frequent calamity of their children falling out of their nests and being drowned. Such is the influence of superstition! for these little hills are believed to be the abodes of devils and unclean spirits, and unless they are consecrated by a religious temple and defended by the followers of Brahmah, it is judged advisable to leave those fiends incarnate in undisturbed possession. I.

3. Aquatic habits of people.

Though the country is at all seasons generally swampy, and intersected with half-filled channels and stagnant lakes, yet in the dry season it is very susceptible of cultivation, and amply repays any labour and expence bestowed upon it by producing abundant crops. The soil is for the most part composed of rich black mould; though occasionally of red stiff clay; so hard and tenacious as to resist the current of the river like rock itself, even when undermined, and thrown down in fragments into the stream. The soil upon the hills is universally

4. Soil.

I. composed of red rich loam, with a sprinkling of particles of quartz or talc; and if we may judge by the exuberance of the brushwood, they also would well remunerate the cultivators. Large masses of granite are scattered all over these hills and seem indebted for their often whimsical arrangement, to some convulsion of nature.

5. Brahmaputra. The intercourse between Assam and Bengal proper is almost entirely maintained by water. There is a free communication between the Brahmaputra and the Ganges, and boats of the largest burden pass by different inosculations out of the one into the other throughout the year. The Brahmaputra may be called the great drain of Assam, and not of it only, but of all the mountainous countries that surround it; the numerous tributary streams of which swell it to a river of the very first-rate magnitude, so as to make it out-rival the great Ganges itself in its tribute to the ocean. History still leaves it doubtful whether or not it receives the waters of the Sampu, of Thibet; though the reasonable presumption is that it does so. Most certainly the Sampu does not flow into the Irawaddi; and unless it flows into the Brahmaputra, and is the same with the Dihong river, it is difficult to account for its course to the sea.

6. Scenery. From the uncultivated nature of the country a voyage up is always a tedious one and as dreary a trip as one could well desire; for days and weeks together nought else is visible but sandbanks and water bounding the very horizon, with no trace of vegetation but an endless jungle of

Bootan & Himalaya Mountains opposite Goalpara

impenetrable reeds; without the shadow of an I.
inhabitant, or signs of animal life but water-fowls and alligators. Though this is the ordinary nature of the Brahmaputra, it is occasionally relieved by groups of beautifully wooded hills; whose shape and colour constantly changing by position, gratify the eye with a pleasing panorama till other and nearer groups come into view. As the voyager advances higher up, the scenery improves; and a series of hills innumerable, retiring far away in fine perspective, till their blue conical summits are relieved by the snowy peaks of the Himalaya towering their icy pinnacles midway up to the vertex of the sky, afford one of the grandest scenes in nature. The sight of a hill in this level land is always agreeable; few things more readily summon up before the mind's eye youthful associations; and the stranger hails its appearance like a friend of his boyhood met in a foreign land. Hence the scenery of Assam is always agreeable, and the eye wanders from hill to hill as over faces once familiar, and with happy invention assimilates them with those of his native home.

A voyage up the Brahmaputra is attend- 7. Navigation.
ed with many obstacles not to be met with upon the Ganges. In the dry season there are no beaten paths to facilitate tracking; the boatmen must either force their way through the high reeds on the crumbling perpendicular bank, or scramble along the bottom; or, what they prefer, keep upon the shoal side of the river, where the sand-bank affords good footing, though with the great drawback of the boat's

I. getting often aground. During the rains the navigation is very much impeded, the banks are overflowed and little or no tracking ground is left; so that pushing along by the slowest of all processes, the bamboo, is the only means of advancing. The prevailing wind being from the east adds no little impediment to the journey. During the cold weather the Brahmaputra is clear and transparent, but in the rains thick and turbid, and at the full flood covered with rafts of pine trees, swept away by its mountain torrents; or by large masses of soil, with the reeds and long grass adhering. The water is esteemed by the natives as good and wholesome, and that blessing is distributed to every village in the country.

8. Route to Bengal by water. The usual route from Assam is down the river Brahmaputra via the Jennai, which leaves the Brahmaputra at Jumalpore, passes by the large town Syragegunge, whence it soon after meets with the Pubna river, a navigable branch of the Ganges. After proceeding up the Pubna river for two or three days the boats meet the great current of the Ganges, up which they ascend for three or four days more, till they come to the mouth of the Matabanga or the Jellingi, down either of which they drop to Calcutta. These two rivers are almost dry during the cold season, and during that period the voyage to and fro is made by the Sunderbunds. Of late years the main channel of the Brahmaputra beneath Jumalpore has been almost shut up during the dry season, and the Jennai is now the principal river. The voyage from Goalpara to Calcutta is performed

in from twenty-five to thirty-five days, and I.
from Calcutta to Goalpara in about eight days more.

There are three overland routes from Bengal 9. Routes to Bengal by land.
to Assam. The first by Murshadabad, Mauldah, Dinagepore, Rungpore, Baugwah and Goalpara. This is the line of the Calcutta dawk, but it is almost impassable during the rains. The second road is via Dacca, Dumary, Pucuoloe, Jumalpore, Singymary, and Goalpara, also nearly impassable in the rains.

The third passes by Sylhet, Chirra, Moplung, Nunklow, Ranneygodown, Cannymook and Gohatti, but from its crossing over the Kassya hills it is impracticable to any land carriage, and beast of burden; nor is a journey performed at any season without much difficulty. Another branch of this road after leaving Sylhet passes over the hills by Jyntia, Hautputtree, Nurtung and Nunclung, and joins the river Kullung, about twenty miles from its junction with the Brahmaputra. This last branch is much preferable to the other and much better adapted for carriage. The principal mode of conveyance is by baskets of the shape of a pine cheese, slung over a Kassya's back, and 10. Via Kassya Hills.
suspended by a stout strap across tho brow. One of these sturdy fellows will carry a maund at a time; nor is he at all particular about his burden; but will take up an invalid upon a chair, and convey him over precipices in safety where he could not venture to ride, and was unable to proceed on foot.

I. Nature has pointed out a very convenient road

11. Via Dyung and Jetinga. across the mountains which could be made as practicable for conveyance as such a hilly country would admit of. The Dyung, a river that communicates with the Brahmaputra, and the Jetinga that flows into the Barak, rise the one on the N. and the other on the S. of the same chain of hills, and both streams are so far navigable that a land conveyance of only six days' march would be necessary to connect them. The intermediate country is so undulating, and the superstrata of rock so friable, that no difficulty would be met with in the formation of a road well adapted for carriage.

12. Route to Bootan. There are numerous passes into Bootan along the frontier, some of which lead direct to the Capital. These passes are called Dwars, the principal of which are Bijni-dwar, Buxa-dwar, Now-dwar, and Char-dwar. The two last are more correctly the names of districts, and are so called from their containing the former nine and the latter four passes into the mountains.

13. Route to Thibet. Thibet is open to travellers on foot from the extreme east of Assam. The route runs across the Himalaya mountains parallel with the course of the Brahmaputra. The journey from Suddia, the most advanced British post on this frontier to Bhaloo, the first town met with in Thibet is performed by pilgrims in about sixteen days. The following are the towns on the line of march in succession: Suddia, Kudgin, Luckquee, Galoom, Mamanoo, Dullee, Omono, Hullee, Sumlay, Hamay, Kum-day, Rheeshah, Bhaloo. About four days' journey beyond Bha-

loo stands the City of Rosheemah, containing I.
fine stone buildings, a large population, and a Government purely Chinese. This route is a very arduous task, the rugged nature of the snowy country is of itself nearly insurmountable, and the hostility shewn by the tribes on the road, to all ingress of strangers, is no less difficult to encounter. The Kangti Chief at Suddia is believed to have great influence with these mountaineers, and is in the habit of giving those devotees, who have the good fortune to obtain his protection, a safe escort to the borders.

There is an open road from Upper Assam 14. Route to Burma and China via Hoo-koong.
into Burma, and thence into China, by which a considerable trade in Chinese and Burmese manufactures is carried on. Indeed the Burmese in their invasions of Assam generally entered it by this route. The line of trade after leaving Suddia passes by Bisa across the Patkoye range of mountains and through the valley of Hoo-koong, to the town of Moon-koong, situated on a navigable branch of the Irrawaddi called Nam-yang. Merchants proceeding from Moon-koong to Ava at once descend the Irrawaddi to the capital; while those to China ascend the Irrawaddi for many miles, to a place called Cat-mow, where they disembark their goods and thence convey them on mules over a range of mountainous country inhabited by Shans (subject to Ava) into the Chinese province of Yunan.

The intercourse between China and Assam by 15. Route from Brahmaputra to Irrawaddi via Noa-dihing.
this route is extremely tedious and can only be followed by a trading people who traffic as they

I. go along. A knowledge of the extreme navigable branches of the Brahmaputra has pointed out a much shorter and more convenient path; and this was travelled over by Lieutenant Wilcox. Tracking up the Noa-dihing which enters the Lohit, the great eastern branch of the Brahmaputra, a few miles above Suddia, Lieutenant Wilcox was able to proceed by water conveyance to within nine days' march of Moon-lang on the Irrawaddi; and this journey he accomplished without any serious difficulty, or any inconvenience more than what arose from the jungly state of the country.

16. Importance of Road towards China.

Considering the small extent of land that intervenes between the navigable branches of the Brahmaputra, and the sources of the great rivers of Ava, of Martaban, of Cambodia, and of Nankin, an overland communication by means of a good road would be mutually beneficial to the three great nations whose territories there meet; and would open a direct inlet for the importation of all the valuable productions of Northern Central Asia. It would also tend to civilize the Hill Barbarians who inhabit these regions; and enable a force to penetrate into the centre of their country whither they can at present retreat before a superior force with compative impunity; and in the event of its ever becoming necessary to take vengeance on the Chinese, an armed force embarking on the Brahmaputra could march across the mountains and enter Yunan, one of the richest provinces of the empire.

CHAPTER II.

1, *State of Country.* 2, *Dynasty.* 3, *Origin of.* 4, *Eminence of.* 5, *Decline of.* 6, *Cause of decline.* 7, *Present Rajah.* 8, *Capitals.* 9, *Disqualifications for throne.* 10, *Rasselass' valley.* 11, *Assam Kings.* 12, *Ahom Language.*

II.

1. State of Country.

This extensive valley, though some centuries ago richly cultivated by an industrious and enterprising people, is now throughout six-eighths or seven-eighths of its extent covered with a jungle of gigantic reeds, traversed only by the wild elephant or the buffaloe ; where a human footstep is unknown, and the atmosphere even to the natives themselves is pregnant with febrile miasmata and death. The ruins of splendid temples are discovered in wastes and forests long since forgotten : large tanks overgrown and chocked up with brushwood, point out the situations of once populous cities : and the furrows of the wild hog or the bear turn up the foundations of buildings unexpected and unknown.

2. Dynasty.

The origin of the Assamese like that of most other races is vague and uncertain, and the traditions extant involve it in superstition and fable. The ancestors of the present dynasty are said to have descended from the celestial regions, at an early age of the world, accompanied with a numerous host of followers, who by force of arms and miracles soon became masters of the country.

II. The probable history of their descent is, that

3. Origin. early in the 13th century they emigrated from some mountainous country on the borders of China, and took Assam by conquest. Having brought no females with them they adopted wives of the country and increased their stability by intermarrying with the aborigines. They were called Ahoms, spoke and wrote a language different from that of the conquered, and had a system of religion peculiarly their own. They ate beef to the horror of the Hindoos, and pork to the execration of the Mussulmen : cats, dogs, rats and locusts were considered as dainties, and spirituous liquors formed an essential article of fare.

4 Eminence. For several centuries these Ahoms held the sovereignty, increasing their territories by valuable conquest, and managing the state with great skill and moderation. The people were brave, powerful and warlike, and during three grand attempts of the Moguls, then in all their splendour, to wrest the kingdom from them, they were repulsed with immense loss and almost annihilated. About 1665 A. D. the reigning Rajah Chukum became converted to Hindooism, and their original god Chung fell into neglect; the nation soon after adopted the language of Bengal, and the ancient Ahom language became obsolete and extinct.

5. Decline. Soon after their conversion the people underwent a total change; and the prosperity of the kingdom began to decline. Family feuds and civil bloodshed hastened their downfall. Con-

spiracy was common, assassination a frequent occurrence; few Princes reigned longer than they could protect themselves from public assault; from the dagger of their confidential Ministers, or the poisoned cup of their favourite attendants, and the whole race degenerated into pusillanimity and contempt. II.

6. Cause of decline.

During the reign of the Assam Rajah Gowrenauth Sing, civil wars embroiled the community in constant bloodshed. Life and property were not safe for an hour at a time; whole families were massacred for alleged crimes of their ancestors, though the supposed offenders preceded them by some generations; and five hundred individuals of rank at one time suffered death under a charge of conspiracy. But intestine grievances were not their only calamities. The savage inhabitants of the mountains burst in upon them with the impetuosity of one of their floods; penetrated to their capital itself, plundered their palaces and temples, and carried of thousands into captivity. To complete their ruin, their avaricious neighbours the Burmese, under the pretext of restoring the state to order and prosperity, established themselves in their kingdom; rioting in the few remnants of luxury that were left to their rapacity; reducing the people to the most abject slavery, or horrifying them by the most revolting cruelties. The consequence was, people of influence and substance abandoned a country so precarious to all they held dear; whole districts were deserted to run to ruin and decay; the splendid tanks of public spirited Rajahs, and the luxuriant fields of

II thriving agriculturists were soon buried in a wild of vegetation.

7. Present Rajah. The present representative of this once powerful dynasty (Sworgo-deo, or Lord of Heaven, as he is pleased to call himself) now resides at Jorehauth in noisy pomp and tawdry splendour, his resources limited to that of a Zemindar; his numerous nobility reduced to beggary, or to exist upon bribery or extortion; and his Kingly Court (for he still maintains his regal dignity) more resembling the parade of a company of strolling players, than any thing imposing or sovereign. His subjects now amount to about 200,000, his revenue less than a lack and half of Rupees, and his army to 500 militia, commanded by a few commissioned Hindostanis.

8. Capitals. The most ancient capital of Assam was Gheergong, more lately Rungpore, was the seat of Government; and for some years past it has been fixed at Jorehauth. Gheergong was a city of immense extent and all built of brick or stone. It stands upon the banks of the little river Dekho, a few miles above the more modern capital Rungpore. It is still the abode of the few Ahoms who have adhered to the faith of their fathers. About ten miles from it is the burial place of the Assam Kings, the city of Azoo. There the sovereigns' remains were deposited in a vault in a magnificent temple, each having his own proper idol buried along with him, together with his ministers of state, his wives, elephants, gold and silver utensils, and a large

stock of provisions, all of which were provided for his comfort in his state of transmigration. II.

9. Disqualification for throne.

I am afraid I have already dwelt too long upon the Royal family of Assam, and perhaps may be censured for introducing such a subject at all; nevertheless I shall venture upon one other paragraph by way of conclusion. A custom from old time existed amongst the Ahoms, that no individual, however near related to the late King, could ascend the throne, if he had upon his person any blemish or scar. He was equally debarred whether it was occasioned by a scratch received in play, a pit from the small pox, or an honourable wound received in action. The barbarous cruelties that this law gave rise to excite our horror and disgust. Kings were torn from their supremacy, and for ever after incapacitated to re-ascend, by having their eyes put out, their noses or ears mutilated, or a finger a hand or a foot excised; and when any rebel faction gained the ascendancy, all the heirs presumptive, and near relations of the ex-King had their prospects for life extinguished by some mutilation.

10. Rasselass' valley.

Nor did the misfortunes of these unfortunate Princes end there; they were not allowed to breathe the vital air like other men; but were shut up for life in Namroop, a confined unhealthy spot, in the most remote part of the country. The inhabitants of this unhappy valley were once very numerous; but like the Princes of Abysinia, many of them have made their escape, and fled to other countries.

II. The following Table, entire, as drawn up by the Secretary Mr. Jas. Prinsep, and published in the Journal of the Asiatic Society of Bengal, for December 1835, will, I hope, be considered an appropriate addition to this paper.

Assam Kings.

TABLE XXXVIII. RAJAS *of* ASSAM—*anciently* KAMRUP.

The best authority is a Native History, (Assam Buranji.) by Huliram Dhaikiyál Phukan, of Goháti. Beng. era 1236. As. Jour. 1830, p. 297; also Mr. Scott's MS. Notes, arranged by Dr. McCosh.—Buchanan is not to be trusted prior to Rudra Sinha.

After bringing down the genealogies to the *Xatriya* Dynasty of *Dravir* (DHARMAPA'LA, &c. who invited Brahmans *from Gaur* to his court, north of the *Brahmaputra !)*

Brahmaputra Dynasty. 240 *years.*

Shusánku, or Arimatu, built fort of *Vidyagarh.*
Phainguya, an usurper of the race of Kumuteshvar.
Gujanke, former line restored.
Shukaranku.
Mriganku, without issue; died A. D. 1478.
Assam divided into 12 petty states.
1498 ——— invaded by Dulal Ghází, son of Hosein Sháh.
Musundár Ghází.
Sultán Ghiásuddín; after whom 12 states restored, of which *Nara, east of Saumar*, has been gradually rising into power, since the middle of the 13th century.

Indravansa (Indu) Dynasty.

1230? Chu-kapha, became independent and spread conquests, surnamed *Asama* (unequalled,) whence *Assam.*
1268 Chu-toupha, son, defeated the Rája of *Cachár.*
1281 Chu-benpha.
1293 Chu-kangpha.
1332 Chu-khampha; valley invaded by Muhammed Sháh, 1337.
1364-9 Interregnum of five years; when the ministers installed.
1369 Chu-taopha, a relation, conquered Chhutiyas.
1372 Chu-khámethepa, a tyrant, killed by his minister.
1405-14 Interregnum of nine years.
1414 Chu-dangpha, conquered as far as the river Kurutoya.
1425 Chu-jángpha, his son.
1440 Chu-phúkpha, ditto.
1458 Chu-singpha, ditto.
1485 Chu-hangpha, ditto.
1491 Chu-simpha, a tyrant, put to death.

II.

1497 Interregnum, and Hosein Sháh's invasion, 1498.
1506 Chu-humpha, a brother, various conquests.
1549 Chu-klunpha, his son, built *Gurgram*.
1563 Chu-khrunpha.
1615 Chu-chainpha; introduced reforms; protected Dharmanárain.
1640 Chu-rúmpha, a tyrant, dethroned.
1643 Chu-chinpha.
1647 Kuku-raikhoya Gohani, dethroned by his brother.
1665? Chukum, or Jayadhwaja Sinha, adopted Hindu faith; defeated Aurangzeb's general?
1621* Chakradhwaja (or Brija) Sinha, built fort of *Gohâti*; Sâmagrya deva, McC.); repulsed Aurangzeb's general called Chukum?
1665 Kodayaditya Sinha, attempted to convert the people.
1677 Parbattia Kunria.
1681 Lorarája; for some reigns confusion prevailed until
1683* Gadádhara Sinha; his son Kana set aside.
1689-1713* Rudra Sinha, built Rangpur and Jorhát; his coins first bear Bengálí inscriptions.
1715-21* Siva Sinha, established Hindu festivals.
1723-26* Phuléswarí, his wife, acquires sovereign rule.
1729-30* Pramathéswari deví, ditto.
1732-36* Ambiká deví, ditto.
1738-43* Sarvvéswari devi, ditto.
1744* Pramatha Sinha, made equitable land settlement.
1751* Rajeswara Sinha, embellished *Rangpur*, allied with Manipur.
1771* Laxmi Sinha Narendra, younger son, raised and deposed by minister.
1779* Gaurinátha Sinha, his son.
1792* Bharata Sinha Mahámárí, conquers Rangpur, and
1793* Sarvánanda Sinha, usurps power at *Baingmara*.
1796* Bharata Sinha, again attempts, but is killed.
Gourinátha Sinha, restored by British; died at *Jorhát*.
1808* Kamaleswara Sinha, or Kinnarám, not crowned.
Rája Chandrakanta Sinha Narendra, fled to Ava.
Purandhar Sinha, great grandson of Rájeswara Sinha, expelled Burmese, and
Chandrakanta, restored, but deposed again, and
Yogeswar Sinha, raised by Assamese wife of Ava monarch, under
Menghi Maha Theluah, the Burmese general and real governor.
1824 Burmese expelled by English.

1712* Date of Manipurí square coins.
1763* Persian coins of Rája Mir Sinh of *Rangpur*.
1780* Bengálí coins of Jayantea Rája.

* These dates are confirmed by coins in Marsden's Num. Or. and others in Captain Jenkins' collection.

II. Ahom Languages. According to a paper in the Journal of the Asiatic Society of Bengal, by the Reverend N. Brown, "The Ahom is a branch of the Tai language, which is spoken, with some variations, by the Khamtis, the Shyáns, the Láos, and the Siamese, all of whom designate themselves by the general appellation of Tai. Among the Ahoms, or that portion of the Tai race inhabiting *Assám*, the language is nearly extinct, being cultivated only by the priests, as the ancient language of their religion; while their vernacular and common dialect, as well as that of the people, is *Assámese*. As the Ahoms once ruled over *Assám*, it is somewhat surprising that more traces of their language are not to be found in the present dialect of the Assámese, which contains very few words of Tai origin," and "that no trace of Buddhism is to be found in the religion of the Ahoms."

Alphabets of the TAI Language

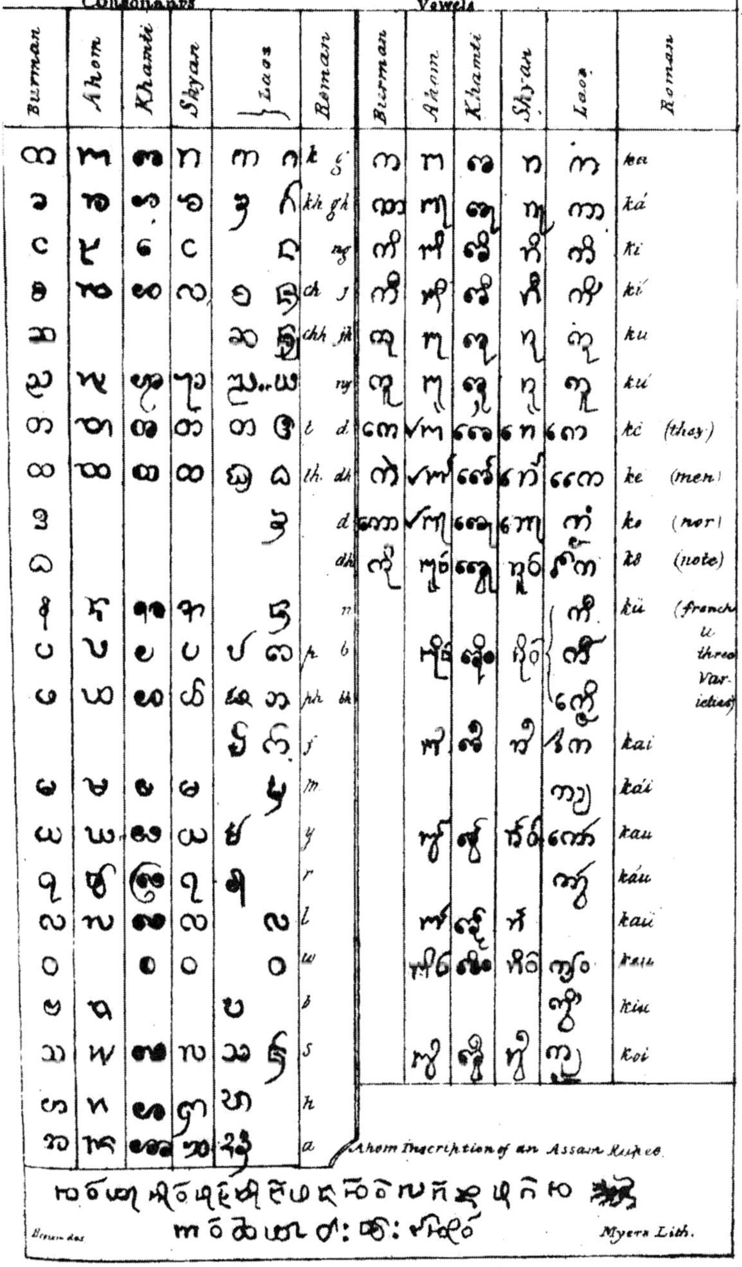

G. H. Huttman Bengal Mil. Orphan Press

CHAPTER III.

1, People. 2, Women. 3, Native Christians. 4, Burmese Refugees. 5, Kyahs or Marwaris. 6, Education. 7, Slavery. 8, Houses. 9, Conveyance.

The Natives of Assam chiefly consist of Hindoos, yet there is a large proportion of Mussulmen also ; but these last are held in such low estimation, that the name "Assamese Mussulman" is a term of reproach. Neither the one sect nor the other are very rigidly observant of high caste principles ; and a greater latitude and toleration exists amongst them, than is observed in other parts of India. A large mass of the population is composed of tribes who originally descended from the Hills in the neighbourhood ; such as Rabbas, Garrows and Cacharies, Kangtis, Mikirs and Miris. Indeed these tribes form so large a share of the population, that it is no easy matter to distinguish the pure Assamese amongst them ; and this distinction is rendered still more obscure by intermarriages with some of the hill tribes. The Assamese have generally been described as a degenerate and weakly race, inferior even to the Bengalies ; but this opinion does not accord with my experience ; and though they are much inferior to the people of the north-western provinces, yet they are as much removed above those of Bengal. They are a shade or two lighter coloured than the Bengalies, with high cheek-bones, and a physiognomy resembling the Chinese. In integrity of character

III. 1. People.

III. they are estimated very low indeed; falsehood and knavery prevail to the greatest extent; they are idle and indolent in their habits, childish and timid in their manners, and perfectly indifferent about providing for their future want. They work for a day or two at a time, and spend the next day or two in listlessness and intemperance; drinking arrak, or chewing opium amongst the women of the bazar. They have the greatest aversion to hire their services; and it becomes a matter of necessity to catch workmen like wild animals, and keep a constant watch over them to prevent their running away. Hence it is often a matter of great difficulty for people not in authority to get any work of consequence carried on.

2. Women. The women form a striking contrast to the men—they are very fair indeed; fairer than any race I have seen in India; and many of them would be acknowledged beautiful in any part of the world. I don't mean Hindostani beauty properly so called; the Assamese women have a form and feature closely approaching the European. In parts of the country not frequented by Europeans, the women go about in public quite divested of that artificial modesty practised by native ladies in other parts of India. Unfortunately their morality is at a very low ebb; and a mother thinks no more of contracting for the person of her daughter, than for a duck or chicken, or renting it at a fixed sum per month. In Assam it is reckoned a disgrace to a family to have a daughter unmarried after the age of puberty; but in the lower castes many

young women do not succeed in getting hus- III.
bands till the age of twenty. It is a very common thing for them to break the bonds of celibacy; nor is the giving birth to a child or two considered any disgrace to them, or any impediment to their marriage. The Assamese women are not remarkable for fecundity, indeed they are rather the reverse. Those who marry according to the laws of the country, become mothers so early in life as greatly to impair their constitution before it is fully developed; and those who are less fortunate, and do not marry till later in life, are by a longer or shorter period of promiscuous intercourse unqualified for procreation. Few families amount to more than three or four, and many of those die in childhood. The Assamese are by the inhabitants of most provinces looked upon as enchanters; and hence the universal dread they have at exposing themselves to be spell bound in the vale of the Brahmaputra. The women come in for a large share of suspicion; indeed they are believed to be all enchantresses, and the influence of their personal beauty is very unfairly attributed to their skill in the magic art.

At Goalpara there is a small society of Na- 3 Native Christians.
tive Christians of Portuguese descent, a remnant of Portuguese soldiers, once entertained by the Nawab of Dacca. They now amount to about fifty or sixty in all. They still adhere to their original religion, and each family has some rude wooden image commonly of the Virgin Mary, cut upon a post and stuck into the ground after the manner of the Hindoos. They

III. have no religious assemblies, nor do they appear to pay any more regard to the Sabbath than the natives. Many years ago the Catholic Priest of Dacca went to make them an annual visit, but that has for some years been discontinued. In dress and habits they are not to be distinguished from the natives. Their occupation is cow-feeding, or that of Chuprasses. They are much feared by the natives, who have as little as possible to do with them. In such a small community marriages are not always to be accomplished amongst themselves; and the solitary party whether male or female occasionally forms an alliance with a Mussulman; but the happy pair are generally cut by both castes. The marriage ceremonies are performed by the Magistrate. I am not aware of baptism being practiced amongst them. They generally assemble at funeral parties, but this is more for the purpose of feasting at their neighbours' expense than from sympathy with the bereavement of the relations, or respect for the memory of the deceased. A great deal of illiberality prevails upon these occasions, and it is no uncommon thing for them to stipulate for certain sweatmeats and liquors and other dainties being produced before they will assist in carrying the bones of their friend to his grave; indeed the authority of the Magistrate is sometimes necessary to enforce their assistance in interment.

4. Burmese Refugees. In an essay such as this, it would be improper to pass unnoticed a small colony of Burmese soldiers stationed at Sinygmary, in the district

of Goalpara. During the Assam war, when the Burmese were in possession of the country, these soldiers were posted in the Fort of Rungpore; but were obliged to surrender to the British troops, with the conditions of being allowed to return unmolested to their native country. However they preferred the clemency of their conquerors to the reception they would most likely meet with from the Burmese Government; and sought and received an asylum in the Honorable Company's dominions; had lands to cultivate assigned them, and an advance of capital to enable them to commence farming. This colony originally amounted to about 500 men, but they are now reduced to less than one half that number. Many of them have died, many others have deserted their old Commander Sham Phokun, and taken up their homes in the neighbouring hills; and the remainder having taken to themselves wives of the country are happy in large families. In any disturbance amongst the Garrow tribes these soldiers are available as a police force, and when armed by the civil powers they are found useful, effective and trust-worthy. III.

5. Marwaris.

There is a very interprizing class of men called Kyahs, resident in the principal towns of Assam. They are emigrants from Marwar, and seem to have been induced to settle in Assam merely for the sake of trading, and so well have they succeeded, that the whole produce of the country passes through their hands. They are generally wealthy and live in a style of comfort and elegance far superior to the aborigines.

III. They of course disdain intermarrying with the Assamese.

6. Education. Education is still at a very low ebb throughout Assam, and that little is confined entirely to the male sex. Learning was thought too dangerous a power to be intrusted to females: and no man would marry a girl if she could read or write. However the school-master is now abroad in Assam, as well as in other places; and a thriving English school under the management of a European, (Mr. Singer,) appointed by Government is now in full play, at Gohatti. Already the number of pupils amounts to more than 100 boys.

7. Slavery. Slavery still continues to a very considerable extent in Assam, and these poor creatures are bought and sold every day for a mere trifle. Every Native on the receipt of more than ten or twelve Rupees a month, has one or more of them; all the drudgery of the household, and the labour of the field is performed by them. Many of them have been enthralled by mortgaging their bodies for a few Rupees; and for want of means of accumulating the original sum increased by exorbitant usury, continue in bondage for life, themselves and their descendants, from generation to generation. Slaves are believed to be kindly treated by their masters; but as might be expected they make frequent attempts to escape. They are valued in the market according to caste; highcaste adults sell for about twenty Rupees, boys fifteen, and girls from eight to twelve. Those of the lower castes do not

bring more than one-third of the above estimate. No slaves are allowed to be exported from Assam. III.

The houses of the Natives are for the most part elevated upon terraces of clay, about three or four feet high ; the walls are made of large trees roughly hewn, sunk about seven feet into the ground, and covered with mats and reeds, and sometimes plastered with clay. The rich and the poor make use of the same materials, with this exception, that the Baboo's is of larger size, with a finer texture of mats and a higher terrace. In ancient days none but the Rajah was privileged to build a house of brick and mortar, none but he could build a house with two round ends to it: and none but the nobles a house with one round end. In order to provide against the frequent fires that take place, prudent persons have a range of earthen pots filled with water fixed on the ridge of the house, and a ladder by which a man may run up and quench the flames with their contents ; or in the event of the fire having advanced too far to admit of any one's ascending they may be broken with a stone, or a push from a bamboo and the water allowed to escape. Many of the houses of Europeans in Assam are built of mat and bamboo. A tolerable one with as much comfort as such a house can afford, can be erected for 700 Rupees, but this does not admit of the security of a wooden door or the luxury of a pane of glass. 8. Houses.

Where water affords so ready and universal a conveyance, carriages and beasts of burden are in less demand ; and so little are their services 9. Conveyance.

III. turned to any account in Assam, that it is possible to travel from one extremity to the other, and not see a cart, or a laden bullock. Man himself is the only means of burden, and while his plough oxen are recruiting their emaciated carcasses in the skirts of the neighbouring jungle, he carries to the market on *bangies* and at great labour to himself the small surplus of grain the fruits of their combined toil. In the navigation of Assam there is less variety of boats, than might be expected, and where the inhabitants are so dependent upon them that a boat is as common to every house, as a brass *lota*, or an earthen pot. Yet the canoe may be called the only boat peculiar to the country. However, many of these are of enormous size, and capable of carrying one or two hundred maunds, though cut out of the solid trunk of one single tree. Such a thing as a sail is as seldom used as a tracking rope or *goon*; in going down a stream, they are propelled by oars or more often paddles, and in stemming the current they push along the shore with long poles. When bulky cargoes, such as cotton, are brought down the country, a common practice is to fasten two canoes together with transverse beams, so that the canoes remain three or four feet apart; the platform is then loaded with cotton or straw, and in this way they admit of carrying a much larger bulk than they could when ununited and with much greater safety.

CHAPTER IV.

1, Agriculture. 2, Rice. 3, Sugar. 4, Mustard. 5, Cotton. 6, Opium. 7, Lack. 8, Silk. 9, Tea. 10, Coffee. 11, Ratan. 12, Plantain. 13, India Rubber. 14, Gums. 15, Ferns. 16, Figs. 17, Creepers. 18, Parasites. 19, Palms. 20, Fruit Trees. 21, Poison. 22, Timber.

IV. 1. Agriculture.

As I have already observed, agriculture is not in a forward state; and though famine or even scarcity of provisions is seldom known yet the produce is little more than the consumption. Immense tracts of country are lying waste that might be under profitable crops, and little cultivation exists but in the vicinity of the principal towns.

2. Rice.

Rice is the principal crop and that is but of inferior quality. The grain is first sown on a piece of well manured garden land, and when about a foot high is transplanted in masses into larger *Khates* previously ploughed, and in a state of inundation.

3. Sugar.

Sugar-cane grows well, but the manufacture is carried no further than the state of *Goor*. There are three kinds of cane, the season of planting is in April, and the harvest is reaped in February.

4. Mustard.

Mustard seed is grown in large quantities, a small portion of it is made into oil, but the

IV. greater part is exported. It is of two kinds, is sown in November and gathered in February.

5. Cotton. Cotton is largely cultivated by the Hill tribes. It is sown in April and pulled in January. A great deal of it is exported.

6. Opium. Opium is an important article and is grown to a very considerable extent. The seed is sown in November. In March when the flowers fall, the poppy heads, are scarified diagonally, and the juice is collected on strips of cloth about three inches broad, and when fully saturated and dried, they are tied up into little bundles, and called *Kauni*. In using it about two inches square of the cloth are infused in water and drunk at a draught. The cloth is afterwards chewed like tobacco till its virtues are extracted. The Infusion of the poppy head, or the powdered capsule mixed with water, is also drunk.

7. Lack. Lack is prepared in large quantities. The insect is propagated by tying small pieces of stick, encrusted with the gum, upon trees proper for their nourishment, when in the course of three or four months the tree is nearly covered with the family. The branches are broken off and brought to the market as Stick Lack. There are two seasons for collecting Lack ; June, and October. The latter gathering is the best. The greater part of the Lack is exported in the raw state—some is converted into shell lack, and lack dye.

There are three principal varieties of silk ma- IV.
nufactured, called *Path*, *Moonga*, and *Indy*. The 8.
Path is of much the finest and costliest quality, Silk.
and is used only by Natives of rank. The worm that produces it is fed upon the Mulberry. *Moonga* is a stouter and more durable fabric than the *Path*, but coarser and less glossy. The worm that produces it is fed on a tree called *soom*. The *Indy* is of the coarsest quality of all, and is used only by the poor; the worm from which it is obtained is fed on the leaves of the castor-oil plant. All of these silks are of domestic manufacture, and are woven at leisure hours by the females of the family. Families of substance have from three to six looms. A small quantity of *Moonga* thread is exported but very little of the cloth.

Assam, with all its wastes and jungles, how- 9.
ever much neglected and abused by man, has Tea.
not been altogether forgotten by nature in her distribution of the good things of this life. Articles more precious than silver and gold grow wild upon its mountains, uncultivated, and till only of late uncared for.

The Tea tree, the identical Tea of China, grows as favourably upon the mountains possessed by the dependent Hill tribes the Kangtis, Singphos and Mattucks, as in the adjoining provinces of China itself, and it only requires the same attention to be bestowed upon its culture and manufacture, to secure the same blessing to our country which has for such a series of years so materially added to the revenues of the Celestial Empire. Tea is the favourite beverage of these

IV. tribes and is constantly drunk by them. Their mode of manufacturing it is not very refined, it is generally prepared in balls about the size of an eighteen pound shot and as hard as a brick-bat, and in this state it keeps a long time. Tea was known to be indigenous to these parts about ten years ago, and during the Burmese war large quantities of it were sent into Suddia by the Singpho Chiefs. I believe living specimens of the plants were about that time sent down to Calcutta by the Commissioner Mr. Scott, but little or no attention was paid to it. How long the subject might have lain dormant is doubtful, had its existence not been brought to the serious notice of Government by the scientific investigations of Captain Jenkins, Commissioner for Assam, and Lieutenant Charleton of the Assam Infantry. The only difficulty to be overcome, to ensure complete success in the making of tea, is the providing proper Chinese manufacturers, and these, I have been well informed, would readily emigrate in thousands from the neighbouring provinces of China, on having an assurance of safe protection held out to them by our Government.

Mr. Bruce has lately been on a tour to the Singphos, and mixed in social intercourse with them. He saw many thousands of the trees growing in their native soils, and brought away some plants and specimens of the leaves and seeds. The trees were of a very considerable size, so as to merit a higher rate of classification than a plant or a shrub: he measured one of the largest, and found it 29 cubits long, and about four spans in circumference at the base.

The distance of the Tea district from Calcutta though great, can be but little obstacle, when such a noble river as the Brahmaputra is open at all seasons for boats of largest burden, even to the foot of the hills where the Tea grows. IV.

10. Coffee.

Coffee could be turned to perhaps no less advantage than Tea, and would require less care and attention. On all the lowland hills of Assam it grows abundantly; and continues in blossom a great part of the year, giving the hill the appearance of being covered with snow. Though but a small plant in its natural state, and seldom higher than eighteen inches, yet when cultivated it grows to the height of five and six feet, and stout enough to form a walking-stick. In its present wild state it is not very fruitful, bringing but few berries to perfection; but by proper gardening it might be made much more productive.

11. Ratan.

The Ratan grows wild throughout Assam, and so luxuriantly as to form the most impenetrable of all jungles. Though not equal to that of the Eastern Archipelago in point of strength and beauty of polish, it is still a most valuable acquisition to the Natives, and when split into withes is converted into every use from that of a rope to a thread, and seems to answer all the purposes as well, and sometimes better. The main stems, some of which are two hundred feet long, though little thicker than the finger, are in mountainous passes wrought into suspension bridges. The

IV. cortex is used for rope in all its uses, and the rind of the spine of the leaves is converted into mats.

12. Plantain. The Plantain is another indigenous product of Assam, and grows on most of the hills. The fruit is larger than the domestic but full of large seeds ; the pulp is however pleasant in flavour, and is a staple article of food.

13. India Rubber. India Rubber is indigenous to Assam ; the tree that produces it being a sort of Ficus Indica. It is obtained by making incisions in the bark when the tree is about to get new leaves, and the juice of a milky colour flows freely, and when inspissated in the rays of the sun, becomes black and consistent with the peculiar properties of Caoutchouc. It is however inferior to the American, being very liable to dissolve to a certain extent during the rains, and become clammy, and adhesive.

14. Gums. Many valuable Gums are found in the forests, the most important is Gum Copal. It is chiefly found on the Naga hills.

15. Ferns. The tribe of Ferns so rare in most parts of India is very numerous, and many of them are very beautiful.

16. Figs. Fig trees form a large proportion of the vegetation, but the fruit of none of them is eatable.

There is a countless variety of creepers upon IV.
the hills, whose beauty and perfume would render them valuable acquisitions to the bower or the parterre. 17. Creepers.

The variety of Parasite plants is numerous and interesting. 18. Parasites.

The Betel Nut Palm is cultivated to a large extent about most villages; the Cocoa, the Date and Palmyra are rare. 19. Palms.

Fruit trees of all kinds, with very few exceptions, do not thrive in Assam, and are seldom or never brought to perfection. Either the roots are eaten up by white ants, or the bark becomes cankered or diseased, or the leaves are gorged by insects; and before the abortive fruit is half ripe, it is filled with worms and uneatable. Even those fruits that might be considered indigenous, as the Fig and the Mangoe, share the same fate with the Peach, the Pear, the Plum and the Apricot. 20. Fruit trees.

One of the most remarkable vegetable productions is a poison used for destroying animal life. It is grown only by the Abors, a mountain tribe, inhabiting the banks of the Sampoo. Its cultivation is kept a great secret, and they carry their precaution so far as to boil it before leaving their country so as to destroy all vegetation. It is brought into Suddia by the Abors, tied up in little bundles, and has the appearance of a small fibrous root. It is prepared for use 21. Poison.

IV. by pounding the roots to powder and mixing it up into a paste with the juice of a tree called Otenga, so as to give it tenacity, and make it adhere to the arrow head. So fatal are its effects that even a scratch from an arrow so poisoned, is followed by almost instant death. This is the poison used by all Tiger killers for poisoning their arrows.

27. Timber. Assam abounds in many parts with valuable timber, not of the ornamental but the useful, order, chiefly adapted for building or for canoes. The following is a Catalogue of Woods peculiar to Goalpara, as drawn up by Dr. Buchanan Hamilton, and included in the "List of Indian Woods collected by Dr. Wallich." It may be considered a fair statement of the Timbers of Assam.

1. Acacia odoratissima. Jotikorai.

   Trunk very lofty, but not straight; often 6 feet in girth: wood hard, and used in furniture.

2. Acacia marginata. Korui.

   5 cubits in girth. Makes good planks.

3. Alstonia (Echites) scholaris. Chatiyan.

   A beautiful tree, often 3 cubits in girth, used for coarse furniture.

4. Alstonia antidysenterica (Nerium antidys.) Dudkhuri.

   A large tree, often 3 cubits in circumferenee. Is considered a powerful medicine. Beads are made of it, to be worn round the neck.

5. Anacardium latifolium. Bhela.

   Grows to a good size; used for making chests and couches.

6. Andrachne trifoliata. Uriam.

   3 cubits in girth; used for coarse furniture.

7. Antidesma. Boro-helock. IV.

Grows in the mountains; 6 feet in girth; the wood used for furniture.

8. Aquilaria agallochum. Aggur and Langchi.

Attains a great size in the low-lands of Assam, and on the lower hills of Gualpara; but in these situations the wood is white, and in no estimation. In the Garo mountains certain parts of the heart of the wood become of a dark-brown colour, and are strongly impregnated with a highly scented oil. When in this state it is usually called Eagle-wood.

9. Artocarpus Chama. Kangtali Chama.

The glory of the forests ot Gorakpur, where it attains a very great size: used for canoes, for which it is well fitted, being both very buoyant and durable in the water.

10. Bauhinia Tucra. Tukra.

A close-grained, soft, tough wood, of a yellow colour.

11. Bauhinia Bacuria. Bakuri.

An open-grained, soft, tough wood; 3 cubits in girth: used for furniture.

12. Bheza Moya. Moj.

A close-grained hard wood.

13. Bignonia Colais. Kolai Beng. Parijat.

Often 5 cubits in girth; used only for fire-wood.

14. Briedelia stipularis. Kohi.

Grows to a large size; wood close, hard, tough; used for chests, stools, &c.

15. Butea frondosa. Polash.

Sometimes 6 feet in girth; wood open, soft, and tough, but not strong; used in coarse furniture.

16. Callicarpa arborea. Khoja.

6 feet in girth; used for mortars, pestles, and common furniture.

17. Calyptranthes. Jam.

8 feet in girth; made into planks, but not considered as of good quality.

18. Calyptranthes. Saljam.

Seldom more than 3 cubits in girth. A close, hard, tough wood, used for posts, beams, and planks.

IV. 19. **Careya. Kombo.**

About 3 cubits in girth; wood close, hard, tough, and strong. Stocks of matchlocks are made of it.

20. **Cassia Fistula. Sonalu.**

6 feet in girth; an open, hard, tough wood, used for ploughs.

21. **Castanea. Golsinggur.**

Branched prickles on the cup of the fruit; leaves entire; timber excellent, close, hard, and tough.

22. **Castanea. Nikari.**

Oak or chestnut; cup covered with strong prickles leaves notched; 5 cubits in girth; timber close, hard, tough; used for furniture and canoes.

23. **Castanea. Kangta Singgur.**

Not exceeding 3 feet in girth; inferior in strength; and toughness to the preceding.

24. **Cedrela Toona. Toon or Tungd; Poma; Jeea.**

5 cubits in girth; a close, hard, but rather brittle wood, of a brown red colour; very durable, and esteemed for furniture. It has an agreeable smell. The wood under the name of Toon, is extensively used among the Europeans in Portugal for chairs and other furniture.

25. **Chotagotadhora, *Bengal*.**

26. **Chryssophyllum acuminatum, *Roxb*. Pithogarkah.**

3 cubits in girth; wood white, tough, used in furniture.

27. **Chung.**

Perhaps a species of Chilmoria. It grows very large, and affords a close tough wood, used in furniture.

28. **Croton oblongifolium, *Roxb*. Parokupi.**

5 cubits in girth; a close-grained but rather brittle wood; used for coarse furniture.

29. **Croton. Lalpatuja.**

3 cubits in girth; a hard close-grained wood, used for small canoes.

30. **Dalbergia Momsita, *Ham*. Momsita.**

Attains a considerable size: wood close, hard, and tough; used in coarse furniture.

31. Decadia spicata. Bongyera. IV.

3 cubits in girth. A close, hard, tough wood, used by carpenters.

32. Dillenia pilosa, *Roxb.* Daine-oksi.

Trunk 6 feet in girth. Wood open, but hard and tough; used for canoes.

33. Dillenia pentagyna. Oksi.

Wood closer, but in other respects very like the preceding.

34. Dillenia speciosa. Chalita.

6 feet in girth. Wood close and hard, but rather brittle.

35. Ehretia serrata, *Roxb.* Nalshima.

5 cubits in girth; gives planks from 12 to 18 inches wide; wood soft and open-grained, but rather tough; not durable; used for posts and other common purposes.

36. Ekebergia. Jiyakohi.

5 cubits in girth; wood like mahogany, very durable, and much esteemed.

37. Elæocarpus. Boropatiya.

A close hard wood, of good size, used for canoes.

38. Elœocarpus Chacrosila, *Ham.*

A close hard wood, used for mortars, chests, &c.

39. Fagara Rhetza, *Roxb.* Bajarmondi.

Wood close, hard, tough; fit for the joiner.

40. Ficus undulata. Bakhalpani.

6 cubits in girth; makes good canoes; wood open, soft, rather tough.

41. Ficus oppositifolia. Khoskadumer.

3 cubits in girth; wood open, soft, brittle.

42. Gardenia. Bonjam.

3 cubits in girth; well adapted for all kinds of turnery ware.

43. Gmelina arborea. Gambhari.

Wood light, but durable, does not warp, and is not readily attacked by insects; used for turnery ware of all kinds, and cylinders of a proper size are turned very thin for drums; other musical instruments are also made of it.

IV. 44. **Guarea. Amari.**

5 cubits in girth; wood close, hard, and tough; used for canoes.

45. **Guarea Gobara. Govorpongyota.**

Used for canoes.

46. **Guarea Alliaria. Bosuniyapoma.**

Used for canoes.

47. **Guarea Gotadhara. Borogotadara.**

5 feet in girth; wood close and hard; used by joiners.

48. **Hibiscus Lampas. Bonkapash.**

6 feet in girth; a soft, open wood, used for coarse furniture.

49. **Jambolifera pedunculata. Holhholi.**

3 cubits in girth; used for stocks of matchlocks.

50. **Kalajiya.**

Common over all India; remarkable for the facility with which it grows from cuttings, and from truncheons; yields much gum: wood of no use.

51. **Lagerstroemia parviflora, *Roxb*. Sida.**

A large tree, 6 feet in girth, and very common; wood close, hard, and tough, forming excellent timber.

52. **Lagerstroemia Reginæ. Jarul.**

6 feet in girth, used in boat-building; but the wood is soft and deficient in toughness. It is extensively used in Bengal under the name of Jarul.

53. **Laurus salicifolia. Horisongher.**

6 feet in girth; wood has a strong smell of camphor; used for coarse articles of furniture.

54. **Laurus Champa. Kurka-champa.**

3 cubits in girth; used for coarse furniture.

55. **Meliacea. Tokor.**

A large tree, used for planks, canoes, and coarse furniture.

56. **Mimusops? Chalpata.**

A tree of moderate size, used for coarse furniture.

57. **Myginda. Silapoma.**

5 cubits in girth; used for coarse furniture.

58. **Myristica. Jheruya.**

A sort of nutmeg, but neither the nut nor mace have any aroma: timber 5 cubits in girth, used for furniture.

59. **Nauclea Cadamba, *Roxb.* Kodom.** **IV.**

A noble tree, 6 feet in girth; wood yellow, used for coarse furniture.

60. **Nerium tomentosum. Adhkuri.**

3 cubits in girth; used for furniture.

61. **Nerium antidysentericum. Dudkhuri.**

Of the same size and uses as the foregoing: beads are also made of it.

62. **Nikari.**

An oak or chestnut; cup covered with large prickles; leaves notched; 5 cubits in girth; used for canoes and furniture.

63. **Phyllanthus? Horinhara.**

A tree of moderate size; the wood used for coarse furniture.

64. **Premna hircina. Chikagambhari.**

It is often found 6 feet in girth; the wood has a strong odour like the musk rat; it is used for making musical instruments, and for other uses. It is said that no insect will eat it.

65. **Premna flavescens. Bukdholi.**

3 cubits in girth; wood very inferior to the foregoing.

66. **Pregulsee. *See* Ehretia.**

67. **Quercus. Tima.**

Leaves entire; acorns covered entirely by an unarmed cup formed of concentric rings; timber not more than 3 cubits in girth; used for coarse furniture.

68. **Rhamnea. Bangla.**

5 cubits in girth; used for chests, stools, and other coarse furniture.

69. **Rhamnus (Premna ?) Gondsori.**

5 cubits in girth; used for canoes and chests.

70. **Sapindacea. Dophari.**

A small tree; used for coarse furniture.

71. **Schinus Niara *Ham.* Niyor.**

5 cubits in girth: a hard, close-grained, rather brittle wood, with a resinous scent; preferred by the natives to almost any other for furniture.

IV. 72. **Spondias Amara. Amra.**

Grows to a good size, but is not made use of.

73. **Sterculia. Bahelli.**

5 cubits in girth; used for canoes.

74. **Sterculia urens. Odla or Hatchanda.**

5 cubits in girth; used for canoes. A coarse rope is made from the bark, which is used in taking wild elephants.

75. **Stravadium acutangulum. Hendol.**

3 cubits in diameter; the wood much used, but neither strong nor handsome.

76. **Terminalia Bellerica. Bauri.**

6 feet in girth: used for canoes: the fruit and bark used by tanners.

77. **Terminalia moluccana. Joynal.**

3 cubits in girth; used in boat-building, as the timber is both light and durable.

78. **Terminalia Hilka. Hilkha.**

6 feet in girth; used for canoes and for furniture.

79. **Tetranthera caduca. Pangch-Petiya.**

6 feet in girth; used for chests and common carpentry.

80. **Tetranthera. Haola.**

3 feet in girth; wood close and soft; used for coarse furniture.

81. **Tetranthera Paromouja. Paromuja.**

6 feet in girth; wood close and soft; used for coarse furniture.

82. **Tetranthera Darodmeda. Vegnal or Bagonal.**

3 cubits in girth; used for coarse furniture.

83. **Tomex, or Litsæa Japonica. Uluyaohama,**

6 feet in girth; used for small canoes.

84. **Trophis? aspera. Saora.**

3 cubits in girth; used for joiner's work.

85. **Uvaria suberosa. Bandorkola.**

3 cubits in girth; a close-grained, soft, brittle wood; used for posts, beams, and planks.

86. Vangueria edulis. Moyen. IV.

A small timber tree, 4 feet in girth; used for coarse furniture.

87. Vernonia. Magor.

3 cubits in girth; used for coarse furniture. The only one of the numerous tribe of corymbiferous plants that grows to be a timber tree.

88. Vitex acuminata. Angchhui.

3 cubits in girth. A very close, hard, brittle wood; used for mortars of oil-mills, feet of bedsteads, &c.

89. Vitex Babula. Babla.

3 cubits in girth; wood close, soft, tough; used for coarse furniture, but in little estimation.

90. Vitex Leucoxylon. Bhodiya.

3 cubits in girth; used in making ploughs; will grow on land that is inundated for weeks together.

CHAPTER V.

1, Animals. 2, Elephants. Rhinoceroses. 4, Tigers, Leopards and Bears. 5, Buffaloes. 6, Cows. 7, Horses. 8, Sheep. 9, Hogs. 10, Poultry. 11, Game. 12, Porcupines. 13, Snakes. 14, Leeches. 15, White Ants. 16, Crocodiles. 17, Tortoises. 18, Porpoises. 19, Fish. 20, Fishing.

V. 1. Animals. Compared with those of most other jungly countries, there is scarcely any peculiarity in the animals of Assam.

2. Elephants. Wild Elephants are plentiful, and move in large herds, and are very destructive both to the crops and to human life; entering villages in day light, and plundering granaries, and stores of salt, of which latter they are very fond. Great numbers are caught every season, and transported to other countries; but the speculation is very precarious, as many of them die before they are domesticated. The plan adopted for catching them is by female elephants, called Koonkis. The females are driven into the haunts of the wild ones, where they are joined by the wild males. In the course of the courtship the *Mahouts* so contrive to shackle the unsuspecting gallants to some convenient tree, that they are fixed to the spot immoveably, and thus are allowed to remain till confinement and want of food render them easily tameable. From 700 to 1000 elephants are exported from Assam every year. Their average value is 300 rupees.

A duty of 10 rupees was formerly levied at Goalpara on every elephant exported. Great numbers are killed every year merely for their Ivory. The Singphos kill them by poisoned arrows fired from a musket, and after striking out their teeth, leave the carcasses to be devoured by beasts of prey. V.

The Rhinoceros inhabits the densest parts of the forests; the young ones are a good deal looked after for transmission to Europe; but they are so difficult to be found, that a party with two or three elephants don't succeed in catching above one or two in a season, and these when caught frequently die in the nursing. The mode of taking them is to shoot the mother, which is easily done by a large bullet, if struck on the forehead, when the calf is secured. Frequently the mother lays hold of the young one with her teeth, and in her dying agonies, lacerates it so severely that it dies of its wounds. The old ones are frequently killed for their skin or their horn. The skin is valuable, and the best shields in the country are made from it. Great sanctity is attached to the horn; so much so that the general belief is that there is no more certain way of ensuring a place in the celestial regions than to be gored to death by the horn of the rhinoceros. These horns are as hard as bone, very stout, and broad at the base, and seldom longer than eight or ten inches, though I have seen some at least seventeen: they have a slight curvature towards the forehead, and in colour resemble the buffaloe's. The horn is not a process of the bones of the nose, but united to 3 Rhinoceroses.

V. them by a concave surface so as to admit of being detached by maceration, or a severe blow. It has no pith, but the centre is a little more cellular than the rest of it. Considering the wild and sequestered habits of these the most retired of all animals, it is surprising how very easily they are tamed. With a little training a young one, a few months after being caught, may be turned loose to feed, and be ridden on by children. They speedily contract a strong affection for their keeper and come at his call, and follow his heels like a dog wherever he goes.

4. Tigers, Leopards & Bears. Tigers, Leopards, and Bears, are numerous, but though the tigers occasionally carry off a bullock, accidents to human life are but rare. There is a reward of five rupees a head allowed by Government for their destruction; certain castes adopt this as their profession, and make a good livelihood by it. They generally enter the jungles at the commencement of the cold weather, in parties of twelve or sixteen, but nearly one half their number fall victims to the climate. The *Shikaris* destroy the tigers, &c. by poisoned arrows. Having selected a recently frequented track, they fix a strong bamboo bow, (a modification of the cross bow,) horizontally upon three-forked sticks driven firmly into the ground, and just so high as to be on a level with the tiger's shoulders. The bow being bent, and the poisoned arrow fixed, a string connected with the trigger is carried across the path in front of the arrow, and secured to a peg; the tiger in passing along comes in contact with this string, the bow is instantly let off, and the arrow is lodged

deep in his breast. He is commonly found dead a few yards from the place where he was struck. The number of these animals killed in this manner is so great, that the amount of rewards absorbs a great portion of the revenue. Every species of deception is attempted by the hunters; old cats with the fur abraded are presented as young leopards, and the naked skulls of dogs and monkeys as half grown ones; some times only the skin of the tiger, without the cranium, and perhaps at another time the cranium without the skin, so that a strict examination, and a knowledge of comparative anatomy, which few but Medical officers possess, is necessary to prevent imposition. V.

5. Buffaloes.

Wild Buffaloes abound in all parts of Assam, they are not much sought for unless by some castes for eating. They are too fierce and formidable to be robbed of their young with impunity; and as they are seldom found solitary like the rhinoceros, the calves could not be secured even at the expence of the parent's life. The buffaloes of Assam are much larger than those of Bengal; the space between the horns is immense. I have found some the extreme spread of whose horns measured 5 feet 9 inches. It is the practice of the country to breed from the wild buffaloes; no males are kept by the feeders; the tame herd is driven towards the jungles, where they meet with the wild bulls which continue in the herd during the season. Of all the animals that frequent the jungles, the buffaloe is the most formidable, and the most to be dreaded when unprotected; and more inhabitants are destroyed by their gore

V. than by all others put together. Buffaloes are kept chiefly for making *ghee;* their value is from twenty to thirty rupees; many of them are sacrificed every year.

6. Cows. Cows are of very inferior quality, and are generally in wretched condition. They vary in price from two to five rupees.

7. Horses. There are no horses indigenous to Assam, but the wants are supplied from Bootan. The Bootan ponies are very superior animals, strong, rather handsome, and fit for any work; their prices vary from 30 to 150 rupees.

8. Sheep. Sheep are all imported from Bengal or Bootan. The Bengal ones thrive well but the Bootan do not.

9. Hogs. Wild hogs are very abundant, and almost all the hill tribes domesticate them; price 2 to 3 rupees.

10. Poultry. Poultry is not very abundant; though fowls sell at 12 for a rupee, ducks 8, and geese 4.

11. Game. Wild game is abundant. Deer, hares, jungle fowl, pheasants, peacocks, partridges, florican, snipe, and water fowl of all descriptions, are procurable, but no game keepers interest themselves in catching them.

The porcupine, the flying squirrel, iguana otter, pangolin, civet cat, and an infinite variety of monkeys and snakes are common to the country.

I once had a pet porcupine at Goalpara, I got him or her (for I could never use the freedom of ascertaining the sex) when very young. It afterwards became so tame as to run out and into the house like a dog, and was wont to make its appearance regularly at meals, and ate from my hand any thing that was at table, whether flesh or vegetable. It had a great deal of comic humour if I might so call it, and whether to gratify this whim, or from love of stolen treasure, became a great thief. Nothing that it could carry away was safe; a stick or a shoe, a boot-hook or a broken bottle, was dragged to its nest, but as it never meddled with any thing that was not on the floor, we were easily able to keep things out of its reach. Latterly this habit became very inconvenient; if any thing fell off the table and was neglected, it was certain to be carried off. On searching its hoard the lost article was frequently found, but I had sometimes reason to think, the porcupine was blamed for taking away things he had no share in. It became the torment of the dogs, and was wont to take a fiendish pleasure in pricking and annoying them. It had a large share of courage, and in fair field was more than a match for any one dog, for it had only to keep its tail towards him to save its head, the only defenceless part about it; sometimes two dogs set upon it at once, and on such occasions it took to its heels, but it only ran to the nearest corner of the room and spreading out its quills, so as to fill the corner, looked back at its persecutors with cool contempt.

V. 12. Porcupines.

V. I never in any of its most fretful humours saw an instance of its throwing its quills to a distance, nor do I believe it has the power of doing so. It has a certain range, probably two or three inches, within which it can strike, and in some cases so severely, that the quill leaves its back and sticks fast in the object struck. This effect seems produced by muscular action, and the quills are jerked forward spasmodically as if by a spring attached to them. If a quill happened to be loose when it made an effort to strike, I could imagine it being propelled to a distance, but not if fixed in its natural state. I remember a striking instance of the force with which the porcupine can wound. A friend was dining with me one evening, and the porcupine as usual was under the table amongst our feet; the Gentleman began to tease the porcupine, when in an instant he changed countenance, and said he thought the porcupine had struck him. He expressed much pain, and on pulling off his boot his toe was streaming with blood. I took up the boot and found a quill sticking fast in it, and on introducing my hand, found about a quarter of an inch of the quill projecting inside. The boot was made of leather, the wound of the toe healed without any bad effects. The porcupine was very cleanly in person as well as in all its habits, and made no distinction between the night and the day.

I have dwelt so much on the history of the porcupine, because even to this day there are different opinions as to his power of throwing his quills. I trust the rare opportunity that I had of observing his manners will justify this episode. V.

13. Snakes.

Snakes of many kinds are numerous, and occasionally take up their quarters in the houses. Some of the largest have been caught in the roofs of houses inhabited by Europeans. The boa, or as some call it, the python, has been known to enter the poultry-house and carry away fowls. Such has been reported to me by my servants; though I have not witnessed it, I think it probable enough. Few of the snakes are poisonous. The wildest natives are aware of the harmless nature of the python. I remember two or three Garrow prisoners bringing a large one alive to me, which they had caught on the hill. One man grasped it by the throat, and the other two bore the weight of the body. They turned it loose in the compound in order to shew its action, and readily seized it again with their hands. I believe they afterwards took it home and ate it.

14. Leeches.

Leeches of several varieties abound in all parts of Assam. The medicinal leech is procurable for about one rupee per hundred, and is to be found at all seasons. There is a species of land leech prevalent upon the hills of Assam. At certain seasons, particularly during the rains, every bush and blade of grass is frequented by them, and it is impossible to walk a few yards through the jungle, without two or three attaching themselves to one's clothes. They are exceedingly small, seldom thicker than a crow

V. quill, and so well armed that they readily bite through a worsted stocking. I believe they might be used for curative purposes as safely as the medicinal leech. I have been bit by hundreds of them, and never knew any bad consequences from their bite.

15. White Ants. White ants occupy a prominent place in the animal œconomy of Assam. In no part of India are their ravages more destructive. They devour the very houses as they stand, from the main posts sunk seven feet under ground, to the last bundles of thatch upon the ridge; and the durability of a house may be calculated by the dead mass of wood, thatch, and bamboo, in its construction; for a house is only valuable, or otherwise according as it contains, a larger or a shorter supply of provender for the white ant. The furniture requires to be constantly looked after; the feetof a table or a chair are very liable to disappear, and whole trunks may be eaten up though no outward signs be discernible. The white ants make as free with the trees of the forest as with the houses; and probably every tenth tree met with falls a prey to their voracity.

The other domestic plagues are musquitos, sand flies, and fleas. Musquitos are not numerous, and for the most part disappear in the cold weather. Sand flies are often annoying, and in spring almost every house swarms with fleas, but these last seldom bite.

16. Crocodiles. Crocodiles swarm in all parts of the Brahmaputra; they generally frequent some creek or bay where there is little or no current, and hav-

ing a sloping shore with a convenient retreat to V.
plunge into deep water on being disturbed. During the heat of the day they lie basking on the sand in the sun; in the evening they return to the river and swim about on the surface of the water apparently in search of prey. There are two distinct species of the crocodile family, the long nosed one gavial, or gurrial, and the round headed one muggur or bocha. The gurrials are gregarious animals and are commonly found in groups of four or half-a-dozen, the muggurs are solitary or only found in pairs, probably male and female, and are frequently found in tanks at a distance from the river. The gurrial is considered inoffensive by the natives, the muggur savage and dangerous, and on many instances they have been known to carry off individuals while bathing in the river or standing on the margin, and even to attack cattle. No friendship seems to exist between the gurrial and muggur: I do not remember ever seeing them in company. The gurrials are much more numerous than the muggurs. Both these animals are easily killed by a bullet if hit in a vital part. The inhabitants of some parts of Assam spear the gurrials and extract an oil from their bodies, and many of them have no objections to eat their flesh. The natives place a great deal of value on their teeth, and believe that one of them worn round their waist imparts the charm of making them more acceptable to the fair sex; certain it is, that it is almost impossible to keep the teeth in the head of a skeleton, as the servants are sure to steal them.

V. Both species possess the means of re-producing their teeth when lost, and two or three embryo ones are ready in each socket to spring forth for use when an old one is broken. It is worthy of remark that the manner of putting forth the embryo tooth in the two species is very different. The young tooth of the gurrial advances straight through the hollow centre of the broken stump and carries it out of the jaw on its point, whereas that of the muggur shoots forth like a sprout on the innerside of the old tooth, and eventually pushes it out on one side by its shoulder. Hence probably a reason why the teeth of the gurrial are so regular, and those of the muggur so much the contrary; the new teeth of the former always taking up the position of the old ones, whereas those of the latter do not. This is a peculiarity that I do not remember to have seen stated in the natural history of these animals, but I believe it to be specific.

17. Tortoises. Tortoises are numerous and of all sizes, from that of a frog to that of a pack-saddle. They spend a large portion of their time sitting on lumps of clay on shore, they are extremely wary, and seldom move farther from the water than they can leap into it at one jump. They are no less timid in the river than out of it, and dive to the bottom on the slightest alarm. Tortoises are frequently caught in nets by the fishermen and form a staple article of food in the bazars. They are exposed in the market alive with their hind and fore legs on each side tied together, they are sulky and fierce in their bonds, and bite any living thing that disturbs them, and woe

to the finger or toe that they once get into their bony jaws, for they seldom let go their hold. V.

18. Porpoises.

Porpoises (Delphinus Gangeticus) (Soos-Nat) are common, their favourite resort is the entrance of some tributary stream into the main river, where they are all day busily employed in pursuit of their prey. They are occasionally caught in nets, more by accident than from any design against them, and are either eaten or boiled down into oil. They are sometimes hunted in their native element by the inhabitants as they would hunt a hog, and the chase forms one of the most exciting amusements that can be imagined. The porpoise is generally attacked in a blind bay or *nulla ;* the hunt is opened by a fleet of canoes scattered all over the bay, beating the water with their paddles and making a loud noise; the instant the porpoise rises to the surface some spearman is near him either to strike him or frighten him by beating the water; away he darts to another place to complete his inspiration, when he is closely pursued or met by another spearman; again he is disappointed in his mouthful of air, and again he dives and rises only to be again tantalized; till after running the gauntlet between the canoes, he is terrified and exhausted; and lies panting on the water, the prettiest mark possible for the spear, and becomes an easy capture.

19. Fish.

The Brahmaputra abounds in a great variety of very fine fish, amongst which are the mullet, the hilsa, and the rue. The sudder stations are for the most part supplied well.

V. 20 Fishing. Fishing in Assam is carried on almost entirely by nets: very few hooks are used. It is either a joint stock, or a family concern. Where the establishment of nets is so large as to go across the river, a great portion of a village is connected with it; but these extensive fisheries are rare. The market is for the most part supplied by single canoes managed by two men furnished with a triangular net extended between two long bamboos. One man at the stern propels the canoe down the stream; while the other at the bow guides the net along the bottom, and when he has caught a fish he shovels it up above water. When they have dropped down the stream beyond the good ground, they pull up their net and paddle up the stream to where they began. Another mode of the triangular net and more consonant with Assamese habits, is to fix it to a frame-work of bamboo, on the side of the river so as to admit of its being moved on a fulcrum like a lever; the long end with the net attached is allowed to sink to the bottom, a man stands by watching when any fish may chance to come over the net; and when a favourable moment arrives, he steps or sits down on the shorter end and raises the net to the surface, when the fish is sometimes taken by surprise and caught. At the end of the rains when fish begin to leave the smaller streams that run dry in the cold weather, every rivulet is stockaded across with nets; only a narrow outlet being left in the centre. In this outlet a bag net is fixed, so that every fish that attempts to escape is secured, and eventually every fin in the nulla.

CHAPTER VI.

1, *Gold.* 2, *Silver.* 3, *Iron.* 4, *Coal.* 5, *Lime.* 6, *Precious Stones.* 7, *Amber.* 8, *Salt.* 9, *Petroleum.* 10, *Hot Springs.*

Gold dust is found in almost all the mountain streams that flow into the Brahmaputra; and even in the great river itself as far down as the hill Nughurbera. That of the best quality is found in the rivers Jengloo and Dikrung, and is valued at 16 rupees per *tola*. The gold gatherers after selecting a sand bank begin the process by passing the sand through a sieve so as to free it from any lumps of clay, stones, weeds, &c. It is then mixed with water in a trough and thrown upon an inclined wooden plane with transverse grooves cut upon it. The sand is thus in a great measure carried off and the gold from its gravity lodges in the grooves. Whether it be that even gold is held cheap when got for the gathering; or that from the gold gatherers in former times having frequently been robbed, or made objects for extortion, they gave up their trade, gold dust is now but little sought after, and those few who still practice it earn but a scanty subsistence from a laborious and dirty occupation. Many of those who still gather, work only at night to avoid suspicion. VI. 1. Gold.

I am not aware of silver being found native in Assam, nor of more than one mine amongst the mountain tribes, and that is in the country of 2. Silver.

VI. the Bur-Kangtis near the sources of the Irrawaddi. It is said to produce about 80,000 rupees per annum; almost all the silver used in Assam is imported from China in a state of bullion, and is afterwards coined, or manufactured into ornaments. This bullion is the only article of circulation in the trade between the Assamese and Chinese. It is a very rude attempt at coining. The pieces are of a round shape, impressed with rude Chinese characters, and appear to have been cast in little moulds made in the ground with the finger. Not two of these masses are of the same value, or size; their worth is estimated by their weight, which varies from 2 to 10 rupees. The hill tribes in dealing in articles of small value chop them up into pieces, and thus make them quite convenient. This *Kucharoop* as it is called, is eagerly purchased by the Assamese hill chiefs, who alloy it heavily and issue it as their own coin.

3. Iron. Iron is found abundantly in almost all the hill countries. It is obtained principally from a ferruginous clay which, after being cleared of a portion of its earthy constituents by washing, is afterwards melted in little furnaces of clay. By this simple process adopted by the natives, four men can fuse about sixteen seers in a day. The best iron is found in the Bur-Kangti country, and is manufactured to great perfection by a wild barbarous tribe called Koonoongs. The *daus* made by that tribe are valued very highly and are of superior metal. Almost all the *Koodals* (hoes) used in Assam are manufactured by the Kassyas.

Coal has been discovered in several places in Assam. Several years ago a bed of it was wrought on the banks of a *nullah* called Suffry, a branch of the river Disung, and south-east of Rungpore. From the inferior quality of the coal and the difficulty of navigating the *nullah*, these works were after a time discontinued. Lieutenant Wilcox discovered coal on the banks of the river Booree-Dihing, believed to be approachable by boats. Coal has also very lately been discovered in the bed of a hill *nullah* that falls into the river Kullung. The exact position of the stratum is not yet defined, but it is supposed to be accessible by boats. These stray specimens though picked out of the boulders of the river are very tolerable, and lead to the conviction that the deeper strata are of much better quality. VI. 4. Coal.

Limestone forms part of the boulders of the branches of the Brahmaputra, above Suddia; being washed down by floods from the mountains. It is found in flat roundish waterworn masses, seldom above a seer or two in weight, and is collected after the rains for sale—about 5000 maunds are gathered yearly. 5. Lime.

A rich bed of shell lime, similar to that found in Sylhet, has lately been found in the channel of a river called Nam-Bur, in the district of Morung, in Nowgong.

Large quantities of lime are made from fresh water shells collected from the lakes.

VI.

6. Precious Stones.

Munkung or Mogaum, in the country of the Burma Singphos, is celebrated for its precious stones. On a range of hills near it, a great number of deep mines are dug, and the working of them affords occupation for many thousand inhabitants. When a stone of moderate weight is found, it is hoisted to the mouth of the shaft by a windlass erected for the purpose. But the workmen frequently meet with large masses, which they have not the power of moving ; and these they contrive to break to pieces.

They begin by kindling a strong fire all over and around the precious stone, till it is well heated ; then they mark out with some strong liquid the piece they wish to break off ; a large stone is suspended from the top of the shaft perpendicularly over the piece to be broken off ; and when all is ready, the stone is cut away, and falling with greater impetus upon the mass below, breaks off the fragment exactly according to the line drawn with the liquid. It is difficult to account for this mysterious liquid being able to prevent the whole mass from being splintered, and how it should preserve such a line of separation ; yet such is the native belief, and it is not improbable that its effect is merely imaginary, or that it is practised from some superstition.

These stones are afterwards cut into convenient pieces by means of a bamboo bow with a string of twisted wire ; the string being applied

Note.—Captain Hannay in his notes seems to think these serpentine.

to the stone and used as a saw; while its action is assisted by some sort of pulverized mineral, (probably corundum.) As might be expected, much bloodshed is frequently the consequence of finding these hidden treasures. When any doubt arises about the party who first discovered one; or about the right of possession; bloody battles ensue with short sword in hand between whole villages. Large stones are allowed to lie around the pits unclaimed by any one: no one venturing to carry them away, lest every one should fall upon him in vengeance. These precious stones are afterwards carried on mules to China, and are sold at very high prices. The Burmese Governor levies a tax of two seers on every 10 that are exported. These mules are driven along in gangs of 20 or 30, the drivers go armed with swords and matchlocks, and guide their beasts of burden by word of mouth. The route they pursue to China is via Catmow on the Irrawaddy. The overland journey from Mung-kung to Catmow occupies about nine days. VI.

Besides the mines of precious stones, there are several amber mines in the province of Hukung, which are wrought with considerable advantage. The amber is cut into cylinders about ¼ inch in diameter, and two inches long, and is worn as an ornament stuck through a hole in the lobe of the ear, both by the Assamese and Burmese. 7. Amber.

Brine springs, from which salt is made are not unfrequent in the Naga Hills. At Bore- 8. Salt.

VI. hauth, in the possession of the Assam Rajah, about twenty of these wells are wrought by the Nagas, the inhabitants of the district. The brine they afford varies a good deal in strength, some wells producing ten sicca weight of salt to the seer of brine, while others produce only three or four. The manufacture is begun in November and continued till April. Being situated in a valley the wells are inundated during the rains. The process is carried on by filling the joints of large bamboos with the water of the wells, they are then suspended in an earthen trough or boiler containing water, a fire is applied to the boiler, the brine of the bamboos is evaporated and dry salt remains. It is remarkable that this salt is attended with so much cost in manufacturing that it is as expensive as the salt imported from Bengal.

9. Petroleum. Petroleum is found in small quantities in some parts of Upper Assam.

10. Hot Springs. There are several hot springs in the district of Nowgong between the river Dhunsiri and the Hills. Some of them are so hot as not to admit of the hand being immersed in them; the water of some is brackish; and of others savours of sulphurated hydrogen.

CHAPTER VII.

1, *Arts.* 2, *Trade.* 3,——*With Bengal,* 4,——*With Bootan.* 5,——*With Thibet.* 6,——*With China and Ava.* 7, *Temples.* 8, *Bridge.* 9, *Bund.* 10, *Fort.*

VII. 1. Arts.

The Assamese are not a manufacturing people; and with the exception of potters and copper-smiths, artizans of all kinds are obtained from other parts of India. Generally speaking every man, or rather every household, builds its own hut, grows its own opium and tobacco, scoops out its own canoe, weaves its own clothes, and plaits its own mats; and from the rude manner in which these are done, but little credit redounds to the workman.

2. Trade.

They are equally ignorant of trade, and the whole commerce is engrossed by the Marwaris. These enterprizing men are stationed in all the principal parts of Assam, and their petty agents stroll about the frontiers wherever there is a chance of making a rupee—bartering salt and other necessaries, for lack, gold-dust, and ivory. These Marwaris must be serious rivals to any European engaging in trade, many such attempts have already failed to establish any profitable agency.

3. With Bengal

The following Tables, as stated in Captain Pemberton's Report on the Eastern Frontier, will

VII. shew the extent of the trade of Assam with Bengal :

Exports from Bengal in 1809.

Salt, 35,000 maunds, at 5½ rupees, ...	1,92,500
Ghee, 1,000 maunds, ...	1,600
Fine Pulse, ...	800
Sugar, ...	1,000
Stone Beads, ...	2,000
Coral, ...	1,000
Jewels and Pearls, ...	5,000
Cutlery and Glass-Ware, (European),	500
Spices, ...	1,000
Paints, ...	500
Copper, ...	4,800
Red Lead, ...	1,000
English Woollens, ...	2,000
Tafetas, ...	2,000
Benares Khinkobs, ...	500
Satin, ...	1,000
Gold and Silver Cloth, ...	1,000
Shells, ...	100
Muslin, ...	10,000
	2,28,300

Exports from Assam.

Stick Lac, 10,000 maunds, ...	35,000
Moonga Silk, 65 maunds, ...	11,350
Moonga Cloth, 75 maunds, ...	17,500
Munjeet, (Indian Madder,)	500
Black Pepper, 50 maunds, ...	500
Long Pepper, 50 maunds, ...	500
Cotton (with seed), 7,000 maunds, ...	35,000
Ivory, ...	6,000
Bell-metal Vessels, ...	1,500
Mustard Seed, 15,000 maunds, ...	20,000
Iron Hoes, ...	600
Slaves, 100, ...	2,000
Thaikol Fruit, 50 maunds, ...	150
	1,30,900

TABLE 12.

Statement of Exports from Assam, and Export Duty levied at the Hydra Chowkey, in Lower Assam, from 26th December 1832 to 12th April 1835.

Description of Articles.	From 26th Dec. 1832 to 30th April 1833. Quantity.	Value.	Amount of Duty.	From 1st May 1833 to 30th April 1834. Quantity.	Value.	Amount of Duty.	From 1st May 1834 to 12th April 1835. Quantity.	Value.	Amount of Duty.
	Mds. Srs. Chs.	Rs. As. Ps.	Rs. As. Ps.	Mds. Srs. Chs.	Rs. As. Ps.	Rs. As. Ps.	Mds. Srs. Chs.	Rs. As. Ps.	Rs. As. Ps.
Pepper,	0 0 0	0 0 0	0 0 0	0 11 8	2 8 0	0 4 7	0 0 0	0 0 0	0 0 0
Mustard Seed,	37,383 29 0	51,402 9 11	0 0 0	83,457 19 12	62,583 2 0	0 0 0	1,52,704 30 0	1,62,704 12 0	0 0 0
Rice,	404 30 0	328 13 9	0 0 0	1,481 35 0	1,302 14 0	0 0 0	5,897 20 0	4,423 2 0	0 0 0
Paddy,	40,536 30 0	15,201 4 6	0 0 0	17,586 10 0	6,594 13 6	0 0 0	8,995 20 0	3,373 5 0	0 0 0
Wax,	8 18 4	152 3 5	42 4 6	46 32 2	865 2 6	234 0 3	29 13 2	597 13 0	146 10 3
Long Pepper,	227 1 4	1,135 2 6	113 8 3	269 32 0	1,487 10 0	134 14 5	504 4 0	2,846 14 0	252 0 10
Munjeet, Duty on weight,	267 39 10	1,339 15 3	133 15 11	1,957 17 2	13,985 5 0	978 11 5	2,042 26 0	12,598 20 0	1,021 5 3
Munjeet, Duty on value,	0 0 0	0 0 0	0 0 0	0 0 0	0 0 0	0 0 0	202 39 0	1,038 15 0	77 14 9
Elephants' Teeth, Duty on weight,	59 20 4	7,140 12 0	595 1 0	134 9 3	13,520 6 6	1,342 4 9	94 29 13	8,828 8 0	947 7 3
Elephants' Teeth, Duty on value,	0 0 0	0 0 0	0 0 0	0 0 0	0 0 0	0 0 0	51 36 0	5,325 6 6	399 6 5
Laba, without duty,	3,063 38 12	36,767 10 0	0 0 0	178 28 0	2,144 8 0	0 0 0	0 0 0	0 0 0	0 0 0
Do., duty on weight,	0 0 0	0 0 0	0 0 0	3,384 19 4	42,236 10 10	2,538 5 9	1,796 6 4	18,157 12 10	1,347 1 10
Do., do. on value,	0 0 0	0 0 0	0 0 0	0 0 0	0 0 0	0 0 0	1,496 23 12	17,947 1 8	897 5 8
Moonga Thread,	69 34 10	13,973 2 0	0 0 0	291 4 0	58,220 0 0	0 0 0	224 21 10	53,889 12 0	0 0 0
Kapass, with duty,	3,726 29 10	16,769 3 4	1,863 3 11	,193 30 0	5,885 11 6	596 14 0	0 0 0	0 0 0	0 0 0
Ditto, without duty,	0 0 0	0 0 0	0 0 0	7,349 8 8	33,071 6 0	0 0 0	6,967 19 14	3,382 12 9	0 0 0
Sundries, with duty,	0 0 0	2,047 5 3	204 11 9	0 0 0	6,642 15 10	664 4 9	0 0 0	8,182 0 1	818 3 2
Ditto, without duty,	0 0 0	513 12 0	0 0 0	0 0 0	913 11 0	0 0 0	0 0 0	889 8 0	0 0 0
Elephant, duty,	0 0 0	0 0 0	5,460 0 0	0 0 0	0 0 0	5,130 0 0	0 0 0	0 0 0	2,720 0 0
Betul,	0 0 0	0 0 0	8 6 5	0 0 0	0 0 0	493 9 11	0 0 0	0 0 0	381 9 4
Dry Fish,	0 0 0	0 0 0	48 0 0	0 0 0	0 0 0	86 0 0	0 0 0	0 0 0	98 0 0
Profit and Loss,	0 0 0	0 0 0	161 1 [illegible]	0 0 0	0 0 0	107 14 3	0 0 0	0 0 0	0 0 0
Fishery,	0 0 0	0 0 0	0 0 0	0 0 0	0 0 0	81 0 3	0 0 0	0 0 0	109 0 0
	0 0 0	1,46,771 13 11	8,630 4 10	0 0 0	2,49,366 12 8	12,388 4 1	0 0 0	3,04,186 6 10	9,216 0 9

NOTE.—The Hydra Chowkey, in Lower Assam, was abolished on the 12th of April, 1835; from which period no duties have been paid on any article of traffic. For this and the two following Tables, I am indebted to Captain Davidson, Principal Assistant to the Governor General's Agent in Assam.

R. B. P.

VII. In former times an extensive trade was carried
4. With Bootan. on with Bootan. At Seelpotah, in the district of Durrung, a well frequented mart was once established. The Booteas brought down from their mountains gold-dust, rock-salt, musk, ponies, woollens, tails of the yak, and China silks, which they bartered for rice and dried fish; but little of that traffic now exists.

5. With Thibet. There is but little trade now carried on with Thibet, and that little is chiefly effected by pilgrims. The few things imported are smoking pipes of Chinese manufacture, woollens, and rock salt. In exchange for these they give musk, ivory, and *Bisá* poison. Assamese captives at one time formed a considerable trade; but since these latter came under the protection of the British, that lucrative branch has been exterminated. During the flourishing period of the Assam dynasty, we are informed, that the kings of Assam were in the habit of sending presents to the Grand Lama; and that a caravan consisting of about 20 people annually resorted from Lassa to the Assam frontier; and transacted merchandise to a very considerable amount with the Assamese. The Thibetans took up their quarters at a place called Chouna, two months journey from Lassa: and the Assamese, at Geganshur, a few miles distant from it. The trade of the former consisted of silver in bullion to nearly a lakh of rupees, and a large quantity of rock salt. This they exchanged with the Assamese for rice, silk, lac, and other produce of Bengal; but this trade has for many years been discontinued.

VII.

6. With China and Ava, &c.

The commerce between China and Ava, and Assam is of much consequence, and is every day increasing. The imports are nankins, silks, lacquered and China-ware, lead, copper, and above all things silver. I have already pointed out the line of communication.

The tribes on the south of Assam all send something or another to the markets. The Munipuris cotton clothes of durable fabric and handsome patterns, the Kassyas iron hoes, and the Garrows cotton.

7. Temples.

The antiquities of Assam are either of a religious or warlike order, and are deserving of particular notice. Near Gohatti, on the summit of a high hill, stand the famous temples of Kamakya, one of the most celebrated places of pilgrimage in India. Thither pilgrims concentrate from all parts of Hindoostan, with confident hopes of their devotional requests being granted, when they might have sued at other altars in vain. The buildings themselves are very handsome structures, on a pretty extensive scale, and would stand a comparison with most second rate temples in the country. But these temples of the present day, composed of brick and mortar, seem only of modern date; and have undoubted ly been erected upon the ruins of a much more ancient set built of hewn and carved granite. These fine masses of masonry are not honoured with a situation in the more modern structures; but are degraded by being transformed into paving stones, steps of stairs, gutters and other subservient purposes. Even in that low state,

VII. evidences of their former grandeur still remain, and a carved moulding, a bass relief, a fragment of a flower, or a frustum of a column, proves their former pre-eminence. So very extensive have these antique buildings of Kamakya been, that the road up the hill, about a mile long and thirty feet broad, is paved from top to bottom with these granite ruins; a work itself of enormous labour and expence. On the rocks along the side of the road several Hindoo images as large as life, are sculptured; but their execution is rude and imperfect, betraying a degree of workmanship infinitely inferior to what may be seen on many of these despised paving stones. Granite ruins of the same nature are to be seen as low down the Brahmaputra as Doobri, about 20 or 30 miles beneath Gowalpara. Poorah, Rungpore, and Gheergong, are also celebrated for their ruins. On the hill of Gowalpara stand or rather are buried some very extensive buildings, but what purposes they have served seem undefined. No mortar has been used in cementing the bricks, but merely the red clay of the hill. It is remarkable that the bricks are quite different in size and shape from any in general use in India, and in all respects the same as those used in England. There are many bricks of a huge size amongst them, some of which may be a foot square and eight inches in thickness.

8. Bridges.

Assam can boast of no less than two stone bridges, the remains of antiquity; viz. one over the Namdung river, and the other over a canal in Kamroop.

One of the most splendid remnants in VII.
Assam is a bund road, or military causeway, 9.
extending along the whole northern border Bunds.
of the country from Suddia to Behar. It is called the Gohaing Koomla Ally, after the name of the Koomla Gohaing, by whom it was erected. This road is about fifteen feet broad and raised about eight feet above the inundation, and when in full repair afforded land conveyance at all seasons of the year. The blessing of such a road to such a country as Assam must have been invaluable. Unfortunately, it is now in many parts lost in jungle, and the rains have made regular breaches through it. There are several other bund roads of this nature, of which the next in point of importance is called the Bengal Ally. It passes through the district of Durrung from N. E. to S. W., and joins the Bramahputra nearly opposite Gohatti. It is believed to have been made by Meer Jumlah, the Mogul invader. One of his standing camps is still observable on the N. side of the road and is called the Bengal Ghur, and a village called Mongul Backa, once the residence of the Mogul General, still retains his name. The Bengal Ally is thought to have been connected with Gohatti by a bridge of some construction or another across the Brahmaputra; thus opening a free communication with the great bund roads.

The many extensive forts scattered over the 10.
country are well worthy attention, but too nu- Forts.
merous to be introduced into a paper such as this. Those of Buddur Ghur, Rajah Ghur and Gohatti are the most remarkable.

CHAPTER VIII.

1, *Seasons.* 2, *Storms.* 3, *Rains.* 4, *Inundation.* 5, *Earthquakes.*

VIII. 1. Seasons. Assam is quite uninfluenced by the changes of the monsoon; the wind blows from east or north-east for more than nine months in the year, and seldom from any other direction for more than a few days at a time. At the commencement of the rains it more frequently blows from the west than at other seasons; these westerly winds are always hotter and more unpleasant than the easterly, and are as unwelcome as the east winds in the Upper Provinces during the hot winds. There is a greater equality of temperature whether during the 24 hours or throughout the year, than is general throughout India. The hot weather is much more moderate and endurable; there are no "hot winds," and a tattie is unknown. The nights are cool and refreshing, and a punkah is seldom put in motion. It must be allowed that the cold weather is not so cold and bracing as in Upper India. During November, December, January, and February, intense fogs prevail, impenetrable to the sun's rays till eleven and twelve o'clock. March, April, and even May are the most agreeable months in the year, and during that season, Assam has the advantage of most provinces. So cool and congenial is the temperature during April that warm clothing is then agreeable.

Very violent storms are frequent during April, VIII.
May, and June; accompanied with tremendous 2. Storms.
thunder and lightning, and hail showers and torrents of rain. Though very awful and frequently very dangerous these tornadoes are grand and sublime in the extreme, and few phenomena of nature excite a stronger sensation, or gratify the observer with more majestic conceptions of the "war of elements, the wreck of matter and the crash of worlds." One afternoon at Goalpara while watching the progress of one of these typhoons, a tremendous thunder clap occurred, as if the electric discharge had taken place where I stood, and I felt as if enveloped with lightning. A few minutes after I heard that the house of a writer, about 150 yards from where I stood, had been struck. On going thither I found that the lightning had penetrated the thatch, descended along a post in the wall, and on reaching the floor had separated into two parts diverging in opposite directions. The mat walls were torn to pieces; every thing in the house was turned upside down; about a dozen yards of earth were ploughed up to a depth of three or four feet; large stones were splintered; and the fragments tossed several yards distant. The hole in the thatch presented the same appearance as if an 18-pound shot had entered, but without any trace of combustion. The writer was in the house while it was struck; and further than being bespattered with mud, and pretty well frightened, received no injury whatever.

The rains set in very early in Assam, com- 3. Rains.
mencing in the beginning of April; nor are

VIII. they sooner over on that account but continue till the middle of October. Thus prolonging the rainy season to half the year. This long continuance of the rains, together with the heavy fog, renders the atmosphere extremely damp and salt, saltpetre and sugar melt and become liquid.

4. Inundation. The Brahmaputra begins to rise in April: about the 1st July, it is swollen to its full height and the whole country is an inland sea; the average rise of the river being about 30 feet. Whole herds of wild animals, no longer able to maintain their ground upon the islands where they had grazed during the dry season, then commit themselves to the tide, and swim stoutly for shelter to the neighbouring hills. It is astonishing how rapidly they do swim; and to what a distance: but animals of all kinds, domestic as well as wild, are demi amphibious in Assam. Yet with all their strength of sinew and agility many of them cross the boundless flood in vain; the inhabitants are constantly on the look out for such prizes; and with well armed canoes dash out into the stream, and spear them before they can get to the shore. Nor is their sport altogether unattended with danger—an elephant or a buffaloe is nearly as formidable in the water as out of it—even a deer or a hog is not to be run down with impunity; the boats are frequently upset, and sometimes fatal accidents ensue.

The rainy season may be called the carnival of Assam; all the labours of the field are suspended; every one seems happy and contented; and lives luxuriously upon haunches of venison, or steaks of the hog or the buffaloe. The flood of Deucalion is in a great measure realized every year. The timid deer exhausted by long swimming and exertion, is glad to take shelter in a cow-house or a cottage. The tiger and the buffaloe swim together in amity, and the elephant and her young with the wild hog and her sucklings. The native anchors his boat to his own roof tree, performs his ablutions on his flooded hearth, and drags his net in his tobacco garden ; where the oxen lately ploughed, they are swum across to higher pasture ; where a field of grain a short time before waved in the rising sun, nought now waves but the muddy water ; the sites of large villages are known only by their roofs above the stream ; and the situations of others are pointed out only by a few palm trees weeping over the drowned and deserted foundations. VIII.

"Jamque mare et tellus nullum discrimen habebant."

Earthquakes are of frequent occurrence in Assam, and few months pass over without one or more shocks being experienced. Between the 1st May 1834, and 1st May 1835, there were no less than twelve earthquakes, the most violent continuing about a minute. The following are the dates on which they occurred at Goalpara: 1st July, 3d August, 6th August, 30th September, 19th October, 21st October, 6th November, 8th January, 6th February, 11th February, 23d March, and 30th April. They all proceeded from west to east with a subterranean noise like a loud clap of thunder. These earthquakes produce the greatest alarm amongst the 5. Earthquakes.

natives ; the moment one is heard every soul rushes out into the street, and a universal shout of terror is raised and continued till all is again quiet. Though very appalling, they seldom are accompanied with any serious damage. They occasionally make a rent in a brick wall, or throw down a piece of plaster, but seldom do more ; however there are exceptions to the contrary. About twenty years ago, the natives inhabiting a small knoll near the hill of Goalpara were so terrified by the unusual shaking of their little hill, that they fled from it for safety, and ran to a distance ; but when they returned, their houses and hill had disappeared, and a large pool of water five or six fathoms deep occupied its place. From all I have been able to learn this story seems perfectly correct. One of the oldest inhabitants died only three years ago ; the pool is still known by the catastrophe ; and makes one of the finest tanks in the place.

CHAPTER IX.

1, Extent of Assam. 2, Divisions. 3, Zillahs. 4, Goalpara. 5, Station. 6, Public Building. 7, Town. 8, Bunds. 9, Suggested Improvements. 10, Chokey. 11, Provisions. 12, Conveyance to and from Gohatti. 13, Post. 14, Temperature and Rain.

IX.

1. Extent of Assam.

The extreme length of Assam from west to east may be estimated at 360 miles; its breadth varies from 20 to 70 miles; and taking 45 as the average, we will find an area of 16,200 square miles.

2. Divisions.

Assam is divided into three great divisions, viz. that occupied by our Government, that by the Rajah of Assam, and that by the dependent hill tribes. The marches between the British possessions and the Rajah of Assam, are the river Galloway on the north, and the river Dunseri on the south, both of which flow into the Brahmaputra; the marches between the Rajah and the dependent hill tribes, are the river Dihong on the north, and the river Boori-dihing on the south. These two rivers also flow into the Brahmaputra.

3. Zillahs.

The British possessions are subdivided into Goalpara, late N. E. Rungpore; Kamroop, or lower Assam or Gohatti; northern central Assam, or Durrung or Tezpore; southern central Assam, or Nowgong or Rungagora. To which may be added the small but separate district Nowdwar or Bishnauth.

IX. 4. Goalpara. Goalpara is the lowest station in Assam, and though geographically speaking it belong to Bengal, yet from its being under the Commissioner of Assam, and being placed on the same footing as the other Zillahs, as well as from its possessing identically the same climate, I shall consider it under the same head.

The district of Goalpara is bounded on the south by the Garrow hills, on the west by Mymensing, on the north by Rungpore and the petty states of Coochbehar and Bijnee, and on the east by Gohatti.

The residents of Goalpara are the Magistrate Capt. Davidson; Mr. Strong, his Sub-Assistant; the Assistant Surgeon; and a Lieutenant Commanding the Sebundies.

Goalpara is the Head Quarters of three companies of the Assam Sebundy Corps. The greater part of the Seapoys are detached throughout the Zillah.

The prisoners vary from 250 to 350.

5. Station. The station of Goalpara was first selected by Captain Davidson, after the conquest of Assam; and is as judiciously selected as could be in such a country. The houses stand on the very summit of an oblong hill, about 320 feet high, and nearly three miles in circumference, jutting out into the Brahmaputra, so as to be bounded on three sides by the river. Indeed during the rains it is altogether surrounded by water, and converted

J. M^c.Cosh Del^t. et Lith^t.

Goalpara.

into a perfect island. The inundated state of the country is the less inconvenient, from the most picturesque roads having lately been cut all round the hill, about half way up, and nearly on the same level; and its insular situation was also obviated by a strong bund having been thrown across a wide nulla, connecting it with the main land. The summit of one of the ridges is cut down and levelled; affording a parade ground about an acre in extent, of an oblong square shape; which adds very much to the comfort of the station, and is the usual place for recreation. The jutting position of the hill always secures for it the fresh breezes of the river; and as the prevailing winds are either up or down the stream, and the reaches are several miles in extent, it is but little influenced by any febrile miasma. The height protects it against the intense fogs that brood during the night on the plains, which at daylight give the country beneath the appearance of being flooded by the river, and which do not ascend the hill till after sunrise. The hill is rich in copious springs of the finest water, but the natives give it no preference to that of the Brahmaputra. IX.

6. Public Buildings.

The lines of the Seapoys run in a winding though horizontal manner along the bold eastern brow of the hill; two terraces having been cut out of the solid clay for that purpose, and at very great labour; for there is so little level land upon the hill, as to render cutting indispensible. This work, as well as the roads upon the hill, was performed by the prisoners; and occupied them several months. The position is one of the most

IX. healthy that could be desired; and the Seapoys are well satisfied with it. There is a well of finest water at the very end of the lines, enough for the supply of the whole. The Seapoy hospital stands upon a small flat near the summit of the hill. The kutcherry, the jail and the jail hospital stand upon a rocky point of land at the foot of the hill, and are also judiciously situated. They are all of them built of the ordinary materials of the country; mats and bamboos; with a stockade of bamboos around the jail. The floors are planked; and raised upon posts, about three feet from the ground; affording free circulation underneath, and yet admitting of a man going under to sweep it. The best of all precautions is taken to prevent the accumulation of filth; a bamboo grating is erected upon a rock in the river close to the jail gate, and the prisoners perform the calls of nature upon it. I wish the Seapoys could be prevailed on to adopt a similar plan for their wants. They are exceedingly filthy in their habits in this respect, and pollute a large portion of the hill.

7. Town. The town of Goalpara stands on a low plain to the westward of the hill. It is of very considerable extent, and has a population of more than five thousand. It has one long street of bazars such as is not to be seen in any other part of Assam, and almost every thing in native use is procurable. The merchants are chiefly Marwaris, as I have elsewhere stated.

The town is almost entirely built of grass, mats and bamboos; and is frequently burnt down.

The Marwaris have fire-proof vaults in their shops; wherein their most valuable property is deposited. With the exception of the principal street the whole town is during the rains flooded with water; the river breaks through it in a full stream, and every house is an island. IX.

The accompanying Sketch No. 1, drawn on the spot, will give a pretty correct idea of the hill of Goalpara, as seen from the north west.

No. 2 is a ground plan of Goalpara, which though drawn from memory, and not strictly correct, will be more explicit than simple words.

aa.	The Hill of Goalpara.
bb.	The Bramahputra.
c.	Nulla, a river during rains.
dd.	A Nulla, ditto ditto.
e.	A Bund thrown across Nulla c.
f. g.	A Bund broken through by rains.
h. i.	A Road round Hill.
j. k.	Principal Bazar.
l. m. o.	A Bund.
o.	A Sluice, through which water runs.
p.	A Lake, never dry.
q. r. s.	Kutchery, Jail, and Hospital.
t. v.	Road to Gohatti.

8. Bunds.

Previous to the formation of the bund e. (see Sketch) the river during the rains flowed in full torrent down the nulla c., and the town was chiefly inundated by it. After this bund was completed, the town was still much inundated; a bridge at o. in the bund o. z. was inadvertently left open, and the water rushed

IX. through it and inundated the town up to the very bund c.: so that the level of the water on the town side was only eighteen inches lower than that of the river side of the bund. On my leaving Goalpara, I believe it was the intention of the Magistrate to shut up this sluice; by doing which, I have no doubt the town would have been comparatively dry, while the rain water might have been drained off by a canal entering the river a mile or more below the town. The bund at c. was begun in the middle of February, 1835, and occupied the whole of the disposable prisoners till the middle of June. The greater part of it was made by carrying the red clay soil from the hill. The river began to rise when about 30 or 40 feet was required to complete it; there was no hope of having time to finish it from the soil of the hill, then become so distant, and therefore the alluvial soil nearest the gap was used. This portion became saturated with water as the river rose, and constant repairs were during the rains necessary to keep it entire, and its head above water. It has since been made as stout as any other portion of the bund. The whole length of the bund, as near as I remember, is 150 or 200 yards. It is in form of a segment of a circle, with the convexity towards the river. It is about eight feet broad at top with a base of equal proportions. I have been so particular about this bund, because, I am convinced, it will add in a very great degree to the health and comfort of the inhabitants of Goalpara.

9. Suggested Improvements. If I were to add any suggestions towards the improvement in the healthiness of Goalpara,

I would recommend that a marsh or jeel marked IX.
v. in the chart, be either drained, or converted into a tank. This is the principal reservoir for all the water from the springs on the hill; it is, in fact, a perfect marsh, and must be a great source of disease. I would next suggest, that the hill be kept free from jungle. When I went first to Goalpara elephants and tigers might have harboured on it, and, indeed, sometimes they have been known to do so; while the roads round it were being made the jungle was all cut down, but it grows again so rapidly as in a year or two to become impenetrable. I would further recommend that the road h. i. along the foot of the hill be raised two or three feet, making use of the red clay of the hill for that purpose.

Previous to 1835 a Custom-House was estab- 10. Chokey.
lished at Goalpara and a duty levied upon all articles of trade, but in March of that year the duty was abolished. This was called the Hydra or the Assam Chokey. I believe all the other chokeys of the same nature were abolished at the same time.

With the exception of ghee, coarse rice and 11. Provisions.
flour, and such articles, there is nothing procurable in the bazars for European use. This remark is applicable to all the stations in Assam, and the residents are under the necessity of ordering almost every thing from Calcutta. Once or twice a year a wandering Jew brings up a

IX. boat load of sundries, and makes a ready sale of them. Ducks and fowls are often not easily procured, and some officers employ a man to go out to the jungles for game, and by doing so can keep a good table. Most residents keep a farm-yard of their own, but in that they are often disappointed, for the goats and cows do not give milk enough ; the fowls give but few eggs, the hawks kill the chickens, and the ferrets rob the poultry-yard ; (so at least the servants say) and short commons is not an unusual complaint.

12. Conveyance to and from Gohatti.

There is a sort of road between Goalpara and Gohatti passable on horseback, but only in the dry weather : for six months in the year, the only means of conveyance is by water. In the dry season boats in general navigate the main branch of the Brahmaputra, but during the rains it is very rapid and unmanageable, and the voyage is performed by a series of nullahs many miles inland, and to the north of the great river. Large boats require six or eight days to go from Goalpara to Gohatti.

13. Post.

During all seasons of the year the post is conveyed by boats : little canoes rowed by only two men. These are relieved every fifteen or twenty miles. The Calcutta dawk takes about a week to reach Goalpara, ten days to Gohatti, thirteen days to Bishnauth, and many days more to Suddia. The rate down the stream is about half that time.

The following Table shews the result of one year's observation at Goalpara:

IX.
14. Temperature and Rain.

1834—35.	Temperature.				
Months.	Minimum 6 A. M.	Maximum Noon.	Average 6 A. M.	Average Noon.	Days of Rain.
May, ..	70	87	76	81	16
June, ...	76	87	79	81	23
July, ...	78	84	81	82	21
August, ...	80	89	82	85	16
September,	77	86	80	82	18
October, ..	74	83	77	79	7
November,	63	76	69	73	1
December,	61	71	65	67	3
January, ..	58	66	60	63	3
February, .	60	73	62	68	4
March, ..	63	88	68	79	1
April, ..	66	88	72	79	13
					126

CHAPTER X.

1, *Kamroop.* 2, *Arparbut.* 3, *Umanunda.* 4, *Assam Sebundy Corps.* 5, *Gohatti.* 6, *Ancient Splendour.* 7, *Aghorpunts.* 8, *Vestals.* 9, *Unhealthiness.* 10, *Causes of.* 11, *Jail and Hospital.* 12, *Improvements.* 13, *Probable change of Station.* 14, *Pay of Medical Officers.*

X. 1. Kamroop. Kamroop, or Lower Assam, or Gohatti, is bounded on the west by Goalpara ; on the north by Bootan ; on the south by the Kassya hills ; on the east (north of the Brahmaputra) by Durrung ; and (south of the Brahmaputra) Nowgong. Gohatti may be considered the head station of Assam ; it is the residence of the Commissioner and Agent to Governor General Captain Jenkins ; it is the Head Quarters of the Assam Sebundy Corps, Commanded by Captain Simonds, and Staff, Lieutenant Mathews. The Judicial and Revenue Department is managed by Captain Bogle and his Assistant Lieutenant Vetch ; only one Assistant Surgeon is allowed for the double duties of the Station.

2. Arparbut. Kamroop, as its name implies, was in ancient times a sort of Idalian grove,—a privileged region for mirth and dance and revelry, and all manner of licentiousness ; and according to Assamese mythology, even the gods themselves condescended to set them example. Gohatti was believed to be a favoured abode of the Hindoo

J. McCosh del. et Lith.

Printed by T. Black Asiatic Lith. Press Cal.

Umanunda

deities ; and yet it appears they liked to keep the Brahmaputra between themselves and their worshippers, and had their secret retreat on the opposite side of the river. Tradition says that in coming down gods and goddesses, to the river to bathe one warm morning, their amorous passions unluckily exposed them to mortal gaze. To hide their shame, and secure them against ever again exposing themselves in such a foolish predicament, they instantly threw up a small rocky island, between their bathing place and the town. But the natives seemed to understand the use of the island as well as themselves, and to this day call it *Arparbut*. X.

3. Umanunda.

In the centre of the river opposite the Station, stands another little rocky island equally sacred called Umanunda, a very picturesque object clothed with trees and crowned with temples. It also is the subject of tradition. In times long past, and when there was very little probability of this island being connected with the mainland, a prophecy was recorded that whenever it were possible for man to walk on dry ground to the Umanunda, Assam would be conquered by the Chinese. In the cold weather this is done every day, upon the sand ; and people's minds are at times somewhat discomposed about the fulfilment of the prediction.

4. Assam Sebundy Corps.

The Assam Sebundy Corps is made up of men recruited from the district, a great proportion are Garrows and Rabbas. There are several Goorkahs amongst them. The total strength is about 750 men. There are generally from 200

X. to 300 Seapoys, including recruits, at the Station of Gohatti.

The average number of prisoners is about 500.

5. Gohatti. Gohatti stands on the left bank of the Brahmaputra, on a plain elevated a few feet above the reach of the floods ; the land gradually lowers as it retires from the river, till it becomes fit for rice cultivation, or sinks into *jeels* and marshes. This plain is bounded on the interior by a chain of pretty hills, stretching from N. E. to S. W. in form of a semi-circle ; with its two promontories resting upon the river, while the river itself taking a bend concentric with the hills, cuts it out in the form of a crescent. In the belly of this crescent, and nearly at equal distances from its two horns, the town and station are situated. The town is of a very straggling irregular form, and almost every house is built of mats and bamboos. Some of the houses of the Residents are built of brick and mortar, and others originally built upon trees sunk into the ground, have had walls of brick and mortar built under the roofs. Three of the houses stand upon a high bank overlooking the river.

6. Ancient Splendour. During the splendour of the Assam dynasty, Gohatti was one of the largest cities in the kingdom ; its fortifications constituted the security of the State from the incursions of the Moslems, and its Government was committed only to the sons of royalty. A small portion of its former extent and grandeur now remains ; its brick, its mortar and earthen-ware constitute a

large proportion of the soil; its numerous spacious tanks, the works of tens of thousands, the pride of its princes, and the wonder of the present day, are now choked up with weeds and jungle, or altogether effaced by a false though luxuriant soil that floats on the stagnant water concealed beneath; the remains of extensive fortifications may still be traced for miles in its mounds and ditches; the gateways of some are still standing; and the guns of others still lying upon the ramparts. Almost every hill around Gohatti is crowned with one or two little temples, all still well endowed, and in good repair; and inhabited by all the ministers and mercenaries of Hindoo religion. In the *Zillah* of Kamroop there are no less than 37 temples, all endowed. X.

7. Aghorpunt.

These temples are prolific in Faqueers and other vagrants who stroll about the country in the most disgusting state of filth and nakedness. Aghorpunts, or eaters of dead men's flesh, are occasionally met with amongst them; during my residence at Goalpara two men of that caste were caught gnawing the flesh from a human bone, and taken up by the Police. They were sent to me by the Magistrate to have my opinion as to their sanity. One of them was not exactly compos mentis, but the other was of sound mind, and told me he had been in the habit of eating human flesh for many years. It was once the custom with these carion cannibals to walk about the bazars picking a putrid thigh bone, with the object of extorting money from the inhabitants, who preferred paying them a few pice to get rid of the annoyance;

X. and it was even considered justifiable to shoot them like wild beasts whenever they were found. One of the above men came from Beauliah, and was on a pilgrimage to Gohatti. The other was an Assamese, a barber.

8. Vestals. There is a temple at Haju in Kamroop, famous for a large number of vestal virgins being maintained in it, in honour of the god, whose duty it is to dance and sing once or twice a week and perform other parts of devotion. There are only two such establishments in Assam.

9. Unhealthiness. From my short residence in Gohatti, I am unable to speak from much personal experience of its climate; but if I am to judge from the reports of the natives themselves, it is the most unhealthy station in Assam: indeed the records of the Hospital for many years past, exhibit a rate of mortality surpassed by few stations in India.

10. Causes of. Few positions could be worse chosen in so far as health was likely to be concerned; true it stands upon the banks of a noble river, but this is comparatively of little advantage as the prevailing wind is obstructed by a high range of hills; and the fitful breeze that ventilates it, instead of being purified by a long passage along the water, blows direct from the jungles, impregnated with whatever unhealthy miasmata it may meet with. Another cause of unhealthiness; is the proximity of dense wooded marshy jungle, and the multitude of old tanks throughout the station, perfect quagmires

and marshes; the very hot beds of disease. From the great depth of the tanks, there is no possibility of draining them; and from their number and enormous extent, the expence of clearing them of floating jungle would be a work of immense expence and labour. The best practical remedy I could suggest to do away with such a source of unhealthiness, would be to encourage the growth of floating soil all over the surface, and keep it closely cropped so as to prevent the generation of malaria. We are aware that the natives of Cashmere convert the surface of their lakes to a useful purpose by first covering them with mats; afterwards strewing them with a stratum of earth, which becomes a permanent floating soil, and sowing them with the seeds of some congenial vegetable. I am of opinion that if the surface of all the pestilential tanks of Gohatti were so dealt with, and the vegetation kept within proper bounds by frequent cutting, that they might be converted to a beneficial purpose, besides being disarmed of much of their pestilential qualities. X.

The jail is placed close upon the river, and is as well situated as the station admits of. It is built of mats and bamboos, and on the same plan as the jail of Goalpara. The hospital stands about a mile from the jail, and has hitherto been built of the same materials, but a very capacious and superior one with brick walls and floor is now being erected, and on as good a site as could be found. 11. Jail and Hospital.

X. 12. Improvement. A great deal has already been done by the Civil authorities to obviate the sickness of Gohatti; much jungle has been cut down, many tanks have been cleared out, the sloughs throughout the station have been drained, new roads and bridges have been formed, and cultivation in the immediate neighbourhood has been liberally encouraged; but very much still remains to be accomplished, which, with the present resources of the station, must necessarily, or at least for a series of years, remain so, and when all has been done that art can do, I am inclined to think that Gohatti, from its unfortunate locality, never can be made so healthy as many other positions in Assam are capable of becoming.

Possibly a time may come when it shall be considered expedient to abandon the present station and remove to another. In the event of such a resolution, I believe that a very judicious place might be selected on the right bank of the river, directly opposite to the town of Gohatti. There is abundance of high land above the reach of the inundation; so far as malaria is concerned the position would be as little affected by it as any place in the country. The great obstacle to a removal of the Head Quarters, would be the sacrifice of property both public and private; and yet there are many examples extant in India of such changes being thought advisable, though made at far greater expence than would be incurred at Gohatti. Most of the public buildings there are of the cheapest and most perishable construction, requiring constant repairs, and to be built anew every seven or eight years. The present buildings will before long require to be rebuilt, and could be erected on a new site nearly at the same price as upon their old foundations. The only difficulty to be got over would be the property in houses of the public Officers, which, as they now stand, might be valued at not more than 12,000 rupees. X.

13. Charge of Station possible.

Only one Assistant Surgeon, with the help of an Apothecary, and four or five Native Doctors, is allowed for the double duties of Gohatti. The Civil charge is of itself unusually heavy, yet he is called on to perform the duties of the Sebundy Corps besides. Several cantonments in Bengal, with such double establishments, and with a much more healthy climate than Gohatti, have two Medical Officers; one attached to the Regiment, and one in Civil charge. If I might venture on an opinion, it would be that such an arrangement would be very proper at Gohatti. This would always provide for any accident befalling any other Medical Officer, for on any emergency one of the two would be disposable; and would obviate the great inconvenience that has of late been experienced, of Sudder Stations remaining for a considerable time without Medical attendance.

14. Pay of Medical Officers.

The Medical Officer at Gohatti has always been placed in an anomalous footing as to pay and allowances. At present, while attached to the Civil station, he has only 350 rupees of Civil pay, and about 40 or 50 of head money for the Sebundies; in all never more than 400 rupees a month; whereas, were he attached to the Regi-

X. ment and ordered to perform the Civil duties, he would have 420 of Regimental pay, and 100 Rupees for Civil charge, in all about 520 Rupees ; and yet the duties in both circumstances would be the same. I believe this latter arrangement prevails at some such stations in Bengal ; and such, if extended to Gohatti, would have its due weight in reconciling Medical Officers to remain there.

In no part of India is the inferiority of pay of the Medical Officer so much felt as in Assam. The other Officers in Civil charge are well paid, none having less than 500, and most of them 1000 a month or more, while the Assistant Surgeon is limited to 350. I have often thought that their pay might be conveniently increased by a Sudder Ameenship, and their time and talent be made much more serviceable to the State. At present, unless upon emergencies, not one-third part of their time is occupied upon professional affairs ; and unless they can draw largely upon their own personal resources, time hangs heavy upon their hands, and they would be glad to be in any way employed gratuitously, to get rid of *ennui.*

CHAPTER XI.

1, *Durrung.* 2, *Tezpore.* 3, *Nowgong.* 4, *Rungagora.* 5, *Now-dwar.* 6, *Bishnauth.* 7, *Prison Discipline of Assam generally.*

XI.

1. Durrung.

Northern Central Assam, or Durrung, or Tezpore, lies entirely on the north-side of the Brahmaputra. It is separated from Kamroop on the west by the Bur Nuddi, which flows into the Brahmaputra nearly opposite Gohatti; and from Now-dwar on the east by the river Burili. On the north it is bounded by Bootan and the country of the Akas Koppachors and Duphlas, and on the south by the Brahmaputra. It is divided into four districts, viz. Durrung, Chootiya, Chardwar and Chatgari, the three first lie along the river, the last lies inland and north of Durrung.

The Sudder Station was formerly at Durrung; but from the position not being centrical, from being situated in a low country liable to inundation and great sickness, as well as from the encroachments of the Brahmaputra threatening to sweep the Station entirely away, the Head Quarters were in 1835 removed to Tezpore, much farther up the river.

2. Tezpore.

Tezpore is situated on a high plain close upon the Brahmaputra and extending a considerable way inland. It is far above the reach

XI. of the floods and fit for the cultivation of wheat and dry grain of all kinds. There are many remarkable ruins near Tezpore, a full account of which has been given by Captain Westmacott in the Journal of the Asiatic Society for April 1835. The Civil duties of Tezpore are performed by Captain Matthie and his Assistant Lieutenant Tucker. No Medical Officer is attached to the Station. There is one Apothecary appointed to it in conjunction with Nowgong. The Medical Returns are made by the Assistant Surgeon of the Assam Infantry.

3. Nowgong. Southern central Assam, or Nowgong, or Rungagora, extends from Jagee chokey on the Kullung river, on the west to the river Dhunseri on the east; is bounded on the north by the Brahmaputra, and on the south by Cachar and Jyntea. The Kullung is but a small river, an arm of the Brahmaputra that branches off nearly opposite Bishnauth, and making a sweep towards the south and west, joins the great river again about 12 miles above Gohatti. Throughout the year it is navigable from Rungagora downwards, but during the dry season it is shut up above that station.

4. Rungagora. The Sudder Station was formerly at Nowgong, but it was removed in 1834. Nowgong was objectionable from being situated in the midst of a bazar, and liable to inundation, Rungagora has the advantage of a rising ground, and being above the floods. It stands on the banks of the Kullung. The Civil duties are at present performed by Ensign Brodie. There is no Medical

Officer attached; the Hospital Returns are made from Bishnauth. XI.

5. Now-dwar.

Now-dwar or Bishnauth is one of the smallest districts in Assam, it extends on both sides of the Brahmaputra, on the north from the river Burili to the river Galloway, on the south from Koliabar hill to the Dhunsiri.

6. Bishnauth.

Bishnauth is situated in the centre of the division, on one of the high plains peculiar to Assam, and on the right bank of the Brahmaputra. It is the Head Quarters of the Assam Light Infantry, commanded by the Political Agent, Major White, who also administers the Civil affairs of the District; the other Officers are Lieutenant Bigge, Adjutant, the Assistant Surgeon Mr. McLeod, and several other Officers doing duty.

I have declined going further into particulars respecting the Stations of Tezpore, Rungagora, and Bishnauth, than was necessary to embrace them generally in a topography of Assam. They are the province of Mr. Assistant Surgeon McLeod, who, I have no doubt, will enter fully into all the peculiarities of their climate and seasons. Probably the time is not far distant, when the Stations of Rungagora and Tezpore shall form one separate Medical Charge. They are gradually rising into importance, and may soon require such an establishment.

7. Prison Discipline of Assam generally.

When a culprit is accused of any crime, he is confined in a jail apart from the convicts till his

XI. cause is brought forward. On being sentenced to so many months or years of imprisonment, he is put in irons heavier or lighter according to the crime, and lodged with the great body of convicts in the criminal jail. The prisoners after their morning meal, are between seven and eight conducted to some public work, most commonly roads or bunds, where they continue to labour till four or five in the evening. They then return to the jail, cook their evening meal, and before dark are shut up for the night. Each is allowed to provide his own provisions. A few pice, three I believe, is allowed to each for subsistence; this they expend in rice and other condiments as suits their taste, from petty merchants in the jail bazar. Those in good health find this limited pittance sufficient, and some even save money, and lend it out on usury. I am inclined to think, this plan of allowing prisoners so many cowries a day to be expended as each thinks proper is much preferable to that of serving out rations. Where rations are served out on a large scale, the contractors are apt to give an inferior article, or in some way or other to defraud the poor prisoners; and even in the event of fair play, which is but seldom met with, the prisoners are liable to be jealous and dissatisfied; but, when they have got the cowries in their own hands, each finds an interest in its consumption; competition in the bazars ensures him the choice of a good article; the idea of being his own purveyor has a moral effect upon his constitution that is of much consequence towards a healthful state of body; and if he is contented with a slender meal, or lives within his allowance, he knows he alone

profits by it. I should be somewhat doubtful XI.
how far the prison discipline of the present day is in all cases adequate to the ends of justice. Many of the prisoners lead rather a happy life, and consider themselves as Company's servants. They take as much pains to burnish their irons as they would a bracelet, and would not choose to escape though they had an opportunity.

CHAPTER XII.

1, Salubrity. 2, Malaria. 3, Properties of. 4, Sources of—Marshes. 5, Rice Fields. 6, Tanks and Pools. 7, Jungle. 8, Neglect of Ventilation. 9, Ruined Houses. 10, Predisponent Causes of Fever. 11, Depressing Passions. 12, Low Diet. 13, Putrid Fish. 14, Substitute for Salt. 15, Impure Water. 16, Bathing. 17, Exposing Sick on river side. 18, Deficiency of Clothing. 19, Prevalent Diseases. 20, Cholera. 21, Scurvy. 22, Sanatarium on Bootan Mountains. 23, Comparative sickness of Gohatti and Goalpara. 24, Comparative healthiness of N. E. Frontier.

XII. 1. Salubrity. I come now to the salubrity of Assam generally, and, as a strong prejudice, has long existed against it, and some Offices have carried this feeling so far as to exact a higher rate of premium on the insurance of lives in that province, I shall endeavour to shew on what grounds they do so. It ought not to be forgotten, that all new countries in India, when first taken possession of by the British, have been found unhealthy; nor have they ceased to be otherwise, till a settled state of the country allowed them to abandon these sinks of human life, the possession of which, in time of war, was of the greatest importance; till too often dearly-bought experience enabled them to select stations more congenial to European constitutions; till the new cantonments were cleared of their native pestilential jungle, the swamps drained, and comfortable houses erected. That this was frequently the case on our taking possession of Assam, the tombs unhonoured, "unlettered and unknown," of many brave Officers in places long since deserted by Europeans afford melancholy proof. Thus Assam was saddled with a name, which even to this day clings to it. It will, no doubt, be urged, that the mortality of recent years, justifies its original character, and the lamented names of Scott, Neufville, Beddingfield, Burlton, Beadon, Leslie, Brodie and Cathcart, will be adduced as evidence incontrovertible. But so far as climate is concerned these casualties might have happened in most parts of India. Mr. Scott died of chronic disease of the heart; Captain Neufville of gout of the stomach; Doctor Leslie died of jungle fever, brought on by a two days' exposure in the jungles at a dangerous season in preparing the skins of two rhinoceroses; Lieutenants Beddingfield and Burlton were massacred by the Kassyas; Doctor Beadon was shot by an arrow, when too eagerly endeavouring to revenge his murdered friends; Lieutenant Brodie died of fever, caught in scouring the jungles at a season of the year when no European ought to be exposed, and without European aid of any kind; and Captain Cathcart of jungle fever, induced by being exposed to a whole day's rain, and being obliged to spend the night without any of the comforts of life. XII.

So much depends upon the selection of a station, that one side of the river may be particularly unhealthy, while the other is the very reverse. At Jogigopa a considerable detachment was at one time posted; but it proved eminently

XII. unhealthy; and though frequently relieved, generally left one or two Officers behind. Yet, on the opposite side of the river is the station of Goalpara, perhaps the healthiest in Assam. That all the stations of Assam are as well situated as they might be, I will not affirm; but I am convinced that, with a proper attention to the nature of the country, to the reaches of the river, and the prevailing winds, as healthy stations may be selected in Assam as in any part of Bengal proper.

2. Malaria. I am of opinion that intermittent fever, and far the greater portion of other fevers and other diseases prevalent in Assam, are the consequence of miasma or malaria, generated in the decomposition of vegetable matter. Indeed, no fact is better ascertained, or receives more general assent than that a certain quality, whether a gas or a vapour, or a film or an impalpable powder is evolved by vegetable matter while exposed to heat and moisture, and undergoing the process of putrefaction, which has the property of engendering fever when brought in contact with the body.

3. Properties of. This miasma is generated in greater quantity in autumn and spring than during other seasons of the year; is more potent at full and new moon than at other periods; and more active between sunset and ten o'clock, than during the rest of the day. Miasma seems to possess gravity, for people that sleep on the ground-floor are more frequently attacked with fever than those who live in the upper stories; and, as I have been

informed by my esteemed friend Doctor Strong, XII.
who has long made malaria his study, that some European cultivators preserve their health in the Sunderbunds, merely by living in lofty houses; whereas, if they slept on the lower story they would suffer very severely, or die of fever.

Miasma is capable of being dissipated by heat; a moist atmosphere is more favourable for its action than a dry one; and a person may sleep in a marsh with comparative impunity if he sleeps beside a watch-fire. Miasma is actuated by the same laws that actuate the atmosphere, and may be conveyed by the wind to a considerable distance with its properties unimpaired.

A ship may anchor a mile distant to windward of a marshy island with impunity; but if she anchors at the same distance to leeward, she will, in all likelihood, be attacked with disease. An army may encamp with impunity on the sea shore of a pestilential island during one monsoon, and while the wind is from the sea; but if the monsoon change, and the wind from the interior blow over the camp they are certain of being attacked. Miasma loses its property of producing fever in its progress on the wind, as if it became too much diluted to take effect; and a town may be situated five or six miles to leeward of a marsh and not be subject to fever; whereas, if situated within one mile, it may have many.

People constantly exposed to malaria become innured to it, and enjoy comparatively good

XII. health, where a newcomer would suffer. The Garrows, one of the hill tribes of Assam, are the most powerful, athletic race of men I have seen in India; yet they inhabit a country, into the interior of which no European could penetrate without the certainty of a most dangerous fever. In some parts of South America when a slave makes his escape from bondage, he finds a safe asylum in some noted malarial jungle; well knowing that his master would follow him thither at the risk of his life, and would rather lose his slave than attempt to pursue him.

Land-holders frequently take advantage of their being seasoned to some marshy situation; by renting their farms at a very low rate, when a succession of casualties to strangers has prevented people in general from having any thing to do with such unlucky spots. In most cantonments in India there are certain marked houses known from their unhealthiness, and these are generally waste, or only occupied for a month or so by strangers. There are generally some good grounds for the reputed character they bear; and though it be a popular opinion, it is perhaps the safest plan to entertain it. The state of sleeping or waking materially affects the disposition to miasma. A person may be exposed when awake to miasma and not suffer, but is much more predisposed to an attack if he is exposed to it asleep; as if the guardian that protected the constitution while awake, went to sleep along with its master, leaving him unprotected. Hence the danger of sleeping in a marsh. Nevertheless a

man may even sleep in a marsh with less harm XII.
if he take the precaution of tying a gauze veil over his face; hence an advantage of the native mode of sleeping with the head wrapped up in a cloth, which, no doubt, saves them from many an ague.

A belt of high trees intervening between a marsh and a town is known to afford a similar exemption to the inhabitants. Numerous instances are recorded of towns being suddenly subject to fever after the cutting down of such belts of trees; and of others being benefitted by having a grove of trees planted between the miasma and them to windward.

If I mistake not the Station of Purnea became suddenly unhealthy from the cutting down a certain grove of high trees in its neighbourhood.

All the types of intermittent fever may be occasioned by the same exposure to miasma. Four persons may be exposed at the same time, one may get a quotidian fever, one a tertian, one a quartan, and one may escape; and the one may be attacked an hour or two after the exposure, another a day or two after, and another a week or two after; the seeds of fever lying dormant in the constitution.

Such are some of the acknowledged properties of malaria.

It is a well known truth that marshes are the 4. Sources of Marshes.
principal sources of this miasma, and hence its

XII. name of marsh fever; that the inhabitants who live contiguous to them are more liable to ague than others, where no marshes exist; that strangers on visiting marshy districts are attacked with ague, that they would elsewhere have escaped; that marshes may be deprived of their miasma by being drained and cultivated; and that cultivated lands may become noxious by being kept in a state of inundation. That Calcutta now is so much more healthy than it was in former years, has been chiefly indebted to the draining of its marshes and jeels, and cutting down jungle; and that cultivated lands may be almost depopulated by inundation, was manifested in the awful mortality from fever, that followed the great deluges of Balasore and the 24-Pergunnahs, bordering on the sea, of recent years; sweeping away thousands and thousands of the population. The station of Hansi, in Upper India, is another instance of the generation of fever from an excess of irrigation. The country around Hansi is naturally dry and arid, so much so that it was found necessary to convey water from a great distance by canals for the purpose of cultivation. Hansi was at one time and previous to the formation of canals a healthy station, but from the excess of irrigation, the country has become a perfect nursery for fevers, and is nearly uninhabitable. Hence also is the reason why the months of August, September, and October, are so eminently unhealthy. In these months the periodical floods are subsiding, the country is covered with sheets of water evaporating to dryness and abounding with decaying vegetation, each pool of which is a source of fever. During these months the inhabitants of many malarial countries fly from their homes as they would from certain death, nor venture to go back till the unhealthy season is over. The Tarai along the foot of the Himalaya mountains, the Runn at the mouth of the Indus, and the Sunderbunds of the Ganges, are in a great measure deserted in these seasons, few remaining exposed that can effect their escape. Many parts of the interior of India are in these months insulated by tracts of jungle, and no one who is aware of the consequence, or values his life, would willingly venture through them. During the months of May, June, July, August, September, and October, the jungles of Assam, are imminently unhealthy, and no European ought, if possible, to venture beyond the limits of Cantonments. XII.

The same laws that operate in rendering marshes miasmatic, also operate though perhaps in less degree in the rice fields of Assam. Towards the end of the rains, and while the fields are still flowing with water, the ears are cropped and the straw is allowed to remain to ferment and form miasma. This is not a visionary idea, for so strong is this belief that rice fields produce miasma that in many places on the continent of Europe, and far less favourable to the development of malaria than India, the laws of the kingdom prohibit the growth of rice for that very reason. 5. Rice Fields.

But marshes and rice *khates* are but two of the many sources of malaria to be seen on every hand in Assam. Every native of rank has a 6. Tanks & Pools.

XII. nursery for fever in the immediate vicinity of his house, called a tank or pond, and every poor man a pit or a pool, which seem as if made on purpose to supply them with miasma, as well as with muddy water and water lilies. I do not mean to attribute any blame to tanks and ponds if kept properly clean; they would then be both useful and ornamental: but from the weeds and jungle that in most cases are allowed to infest them, they exert the most baneful effects on the constitution of the inhabitants. If the ditches of Fort William were allowed to remain filled with stagnant water, and become a field for studying the botany of reeds and rushes, its present healthy character would speedily leave it; and were the numerous tanks throughout Calcutta, left to nature to overgrow with weeds, the consequences would be truly melancholy.

7. Jungle. Another hot bed of malaria is the quantity of underwood and jungle with which most native habitations are choked up, so impenetrable as to form a barrier to all encroachment from without, and a screen through which the eye of curiosity cannot penetrate. But this belt of jungle is also the seat of malaria, and the better it answers the purpose intended by its owners, the more concentrated is the malaria which the dense mass of vegetables that die every season engenders. These belts of jungle are pregnant with another evil; they are the usual resort for performing the calls of nature, and the effluvia from the daily deposit of so much filthiness comes in for a large share of the illness entailed upon the household.

Another cause of fever is the total disregard to ventilation in native houses. It is well known that a close confined atmosphere is the most favourable place for the action of malaria, and that nothing dissipates it so readily as a current of fresh air, but in native houses the doors are few, the windows still fewer, and both seem constructed on purpose to admit as little of the vital air as is consistent with the smallest possible quantity of light; and these are for the most part obstructed with mats or screens. Moreover, the premises are frequently surrounded by a lofty wall or matting, which with the trees outside, render it almost a matter of impossibility for any useful ventilation to take place. This same obstruction to ventilation is seen on the grand scale around almost every town in Bengal. The suburbs of every large city resembles a dense forest more than a habitation proper for human beings. Even the City of Calcutta is surrounded with a cordon of populated jungle that must be obnoxious to the inhabitants of its palaces, and the salt-water lake may be considered as a grand depot of fever. XII. 8. Neglect of Ventilation.

Another cause of miasma is the quantity of ruined houses, and deserted grounds around the ruins, with obstructed drains and decaying trees. I am afraid these are but too little thought of as injurious, even by a European Police. 9. Ruined Houses.

Having stated the principal sources of malaria I shall next mention a few of the many causes that render the constitution susceptible of its 10. Predisponent Causes of Fever.

XII. action. A sound mind in a sound body has long been acknowledged to be the best safeguard against malaria; a man in good health and of a cheerful frame of mind may be many times exposed to the influence of fever with impunity; whereas if labouring under any bodily ailment or depressing passion, he is very liable to catch disease. Hence poor diet, bad water, scanty clothing, wretched houses, famine, fatigue, melancholy, prepare the body for the seeds of fever; and the weak and inanimate are more frequently victims than the strong and the active.

11. Depressing Passions.

12. Low Diet.

The exceedingly low rate of living among the poorer classes strongly predisposes to fever. I wish I could as easily point out how it could be amended as demonstrate its hurtful effects. Many of the articles of diet are very objectionable either from the material itself, the manner of preparing it, or its mode of cooking.

13. Putrid Fish.

None is so deleterious as the half cured, or wholly putrid fish, so much in use by the poor. Fish prepared in this manner require little salt, and go a great way farther than if fresh or properly cured; but in proportion as they spare the price of the individual they sow the seeds of disease in his frame. Raw rice, under-baked bread, raw green fruits, deficiency of salt, and the inveterate practice amongst the Assamese of eating opium, must have a powerful effect in lowering the tone of the constitution.

The poorer classes cannot afford the luxury of salt, and are in the habit of using wood-ashes as a substitute. XII. 14. Substitute for Salt.

No part of diet is more frequently at fault than the water used for drink. One would expect that the Natives of Assam, in common with other parts of India, so excessively careful of defilement in their manner of eating and drinking, would be very particular about their water their only beverage; and that nothing less than the produce of the crystal spring, or rain water in all its purity as it fell from the clouds, would satisfy them. But no nation I have ever seen are so notoriously indifferent about the water they drink. If we visit any of the legitimate places for lifting water, any of the ghauts on the river, we will see a dense mass of naked people of all sexes and sizes, standing up to their middles in water; some washing their clothes, some their bodies, and all of them stirring up as much mud from the bottom as they can, yet when their ablutions are completed, filling their pitchers where they stand for the day's consumption: probably, one of the common sewers of the bazar enters the river a few yards above the ghaut; it may happen that the surface of the water is strewed with the yet warm ashes of some lately incinerated human being, or that a putrifying carcase is revolving in an adjacent eddy. If we visit any of the private tanks, we will see a spacious pool of water shaded with tall trees, and garnished with weeds; the necessary reservoir of all the surface water of the neighbourhood; a perfect 15. Impure Water.

XII. infusion of every thing offensive and filthy about the place; and literally alive with animalculæ; here too we shall see the same scene of washing clothes, and scrubbing bodies, and other acts of uncleanliness. Yet from this same pool they draw their daily supply of water; and wonder that they should become sick from using it.

16. Bathing. The universal practice of bathing prevalent in Assam has, I have no doubt, a bad effect upon the health of the people. In a country, such as India, where so much of the body is exposed naked to the accumulation of dust and clamminess of perspiration it was no doubt a wise and provident law that instituted ablution as a religious rite; for no other plan so effectual could have been devised, to ensure cleanliness and a healthy state of skin. But I am afraid that bathing is often abused, that it is considered in the light of an ordinance of their religion, and is practised because people think it ought to be practised, without any regard to the season of the year, the state of the weather, or the condition of the body, as to health or disease. There no doubt are cold raw rainy days in the summer season, and bleak withering days in winter, when people even in good health would be much better in their beds at home than doing penance on the banks of a river; and a person labouring under diarrhœa, or dysentery, or internal inflammation of any kind, or under the influence of mercury, would be committing an act of great indiscretion in taking a cold bath. Yet we know that people do bathe every day while so affected.

XII.

17. Exposing Sick on river side.

Ill-timed bathing is not the only instance of the religious laws of the country aggravating the diseases of the people and adding to the bills of mortality. The Hindoo practice of hurrying persons, dangerously ill, to the banks of the river and exposing them in the open air with their feet immersed in the water, and their body besmeared with the slime of the river till the ordeal puts an end to their existence, must be considered as a frequent cause of death.

There is no doubt that thousands of lives are by this treatment taken away, that with proper care and nursing would have recovered. This custom equally repugnant to human nature with Suttee-ism is probably ten times more destructive to human life. Where one person's death was caused by Suttee-ism ten deaths may be caused by this abhorred custom. The friends of a poor dependant unfortunate widow, incited her to the commission of suicide in order to rid themselves of a relation who might claim a maintenance amongst them: the friends of a person dangerously ill take advantages of his helplessness, and hurry him out of the world, to rid themselves of a disagreeable acquaintance, or possess themselves of his inheritance: and if it should so happen that his constitution support him through this trial and he recover, he is looked upon as an outcast and a vagabond, because he did not die.

We hear of human sacrifices in Goomsur and other wild and barbarous places, and wonder that the earth does not gape and swallow

XII. up alive the blood-stained murderer: but we forget that in the most populous cities in India, even in the City of Calcutta, sacrifices of life no less atrocious in the eyes of humanity, are every day perpetrated. We have only to go to any of the *Murda Ghauts*, where we shall see the old, the young and the middle aged dragged away in the extremity of sickness from their homes, their families and their comforts, when such were most wanted; and exposed on the river side on a *charpoy* with only two or three cold-blooded hired attendants preparing their funeral pile, and watching when the vital spark shall be extinguished.

Though there is no use in adducing proofs to confirm this assertion, yet the following case is so applicable to that purpose that I shall perhaps be excused for inserting it. On an evening of January last I accompanied a Medical friend in a visit to a native lady of rank that had had a miscarriage that day at noon. We found her shut up in a close confined dark room, hot and suffocating almost beyond our indurance, and crammed full with attendants. The patient was a young woman to all appearance lately in good health. She had had no flooding and the placenta came away in the natural manner. She lay quite insensible, breathing short and laborious, pulse not to be felt even in the humeral artery, eyes fixed and open, skin of natural temperature. After prescribing for her and enjoining perfect quietness and rest we went away intending to return in an hour or two. About ten, when we called at the house, we learned that they had carried her off to the river side, where she soon after expired. I have not a doubt that if this woman had been allowed to lie quietly upon her back in her room that she might have recovered. In her condition it was dangerous even to raise her, nevertheless she was placed upon a bed, carried through a labyrinth of narrow passages and stair cases out of a very hot room into a cold atmosphere, and jolted along through the streets on men's heads to the *murda ghaut*, enough to cause the death of any one in such a condition. XII.

18. Deficiency of Clothing.

The scantiness of clothing, customary amongst the natives, strongly predisposes to fever; they have no adequate protection against the cold weather, and suffer most severely from the mornings and evenings. During the rains the Assamese wear what they call *jampies*, a sort of broad brimmed hat, about three feet in diameter, made of mats and split bamboos. This is one of the most sensible articles in dress that they have, but it is no uncommon thing for them to strip off the most part of their clothes during a shower, and stow them in the crown of the *jampy* till the rain is over.

19. Prevalent Diseases.

The most prevalent diseases amongst the Seapoys at Goalpara and Gohatti are intermittent fever and syphilis. This last disease is extremely common, and I have frequently had more men laid up by it than by all others put together. Gonorrhœa was comparatively rare; buboes in the groins were common at Goalpara, and often without any apparent cause; erup-

XII. tions on the skin, itch, and ring-worm were very prevalent. Continued fever was rare, elephantiasis and goitre were hardly known, and leprosy but seldom seen.

Amongst the prisoners intermittent fever, dysentery, diarrhaea, and rheumatism were most frequent, and even amongst them continued fever was rare. I have seen but very little of small pox in Assam, though it every fourth or fifth year breaks out with great virulence. Inoculation with the small pox virus is practised by the natives; they have a strong prejudice against vaccination, this aversion to it is peculiar to the people of the plains; those of the hills are very willing to have it performed.

20. Cholera. Cholera, though not of every year's occurrence, occasionally breaks out with fearful violence. In May and June 1834, a large portion of the population of Assam was swept away by it. In the town of Goalpara alone, with a population of about 5,000, upwards of three hundred died of it. The natives that lived on the hill were comparatively exempt from it or had it in a milder form; this exemption has always been observed on previous visitations of Cholera. In 1834, Cholera continued to rage for about six weeks; its progress up the Brahmaputra was very well marked though slow. I first heard of its being at Dacca, some time after at Jumalpore, next it reached Goalpara, then it proceeded to Gohatti, and thence to Bishnauth, and all in regular succession. Its virulence seemed to have abated at Bishnauth, where only a small proportion died

of it. Several weeks elapsed during its progress from Dacca to Bishnauth. XII.

On my assuming Medical charge of Gohatti, I was surprised to find scurvy endemic amongst the prisoners, and that many of them had lately died of it. The mouth was the chief seat of the disease. It manifested itself first by a sponginess of the gums and looseness of the teeth, or by a foul ulcer inside the cheek : all the symptoms of profuse salivation rapidly ensued, the gums became a mass of suppurating matter, the teeth dropped out, the ulcers spread all over the mouth, the cheeks sloughed away, the patient sank exhausted, or if he recovered he was frightfully deformed. The Hospital stores contained almost no antiscorbutic. Oranges and lemons (indigenous to the Kassya Hills,) were then plentiful in the bazar, I ordered them to bought up in basket fulls. I prescribed them ad libitum in every case and found them a perfect specific. I was fortunate in losing only one or two cases, and these were far advanced before they came under my care. 21. Scurvy.

I cannot omit this opportunity of remarking that while a Sanatarium for the Lower Provinces has so long been sought for, and is even to this day a desideratum, that the frontier of Bootan should be overlooked. At this moment (20th September), while overcome with the oppressive heat and moisture of a low country flowing with water, I am looking out upon the mountains of Bootan capped with newly fallen snow. These mountains run along the whole frontier of Assam, and may be 22. Sanatarium on Bootan Mountains.

XII. approached by many tributary branches of the Brahmaputra to within 15 or 20 miles, or less, of their base. The country between the extreme branches of these rivers and the hills is so level, that an excellent road could be made, with little difficulty or expence to the base of the hills; and the hills themselves rise so abruptly from the plain that the ascent could be made in a few hours. The only difficulty to be surmounted would be to obtain the consent of the jealous Bootan Government to a grant of one of their hill tops, with a right of open communication to and from it. There could be nothing unreasonable on the part of Government in making such a demand, and no real cause for jealousy on the part of the Booteas; for by an accommodation exactly similar and of the very utmost importance to these Mountaineers, they are allowed to hold extensive lands called dwars in the plains for the purpose of growing rice, for which their hills are not adapted; they paying a tribute merely nominal for the privilege.

I am fully convinced that a Sanatarium affording all the coldness and salubrity of Simla itself, and that congeniality of climate adapted to the restoration of a European constitution when broken by tropical disease, or worn out by a long residence in India, could be selected in that mountain range; and that it only requires encouragement to become the Mount Pelier of the Lower Provinces. The voyage thither from Calcutta and all parts on the Ganges as high as Patna, could easily be performed even by the present mode of navigation, in from 24 to 30 days, and by steam in about one-third of that time. Hundreds of valuable lives could be recruited there that must necessarily become extinct on a six months' voyage to Simla; and hundreds more who could not afford the very exorbitant charge of 240 Rs. a month for their accommodation on board a pilot schooner, or the little less heavy expences of a voyage to the Cape or New South Wales, could step into a comfortable boat, and be conveyed in a short time to a healthy climate at little more expenditure than the rate of living with their regiment. XII.

Darjiling, at present under examination as a Sanatarium, is situated on this same chain of hills.

Before any material improvement in the salubrity of Assam can be effected, it will be necessary to cut down and clear away the noxious jungle, to reclaim its waste lands by cultivation, to drain its marshes, to clear out its tanks, to build the houses upon the hills, to abolish the use of opium, and be guided by the laws that generate and spread malaria.

The following Table as extracted from the Records of the Medical Board, will shew the comparative mortality amongst the Prisoners at Goalpara and Gohatti, for 1833:

Name of the Station.	Average strength, during the four quarters of the year.	Average admission, during the four quarters of the year.	Proportion of sick to strength.	Deaths by ordinary diseases, during the four quarters.	Deaths by Cholera Morbus, during the four quarters.	Ratio per cent. of deaths from ordinary diseases.	Ratio per cent of deaths from Cholera Morbus.	General ratio per cent.
Goalpara,	342	79	1 to 5	10	"	2·95	"	2·95
Gohatti,	474	104	1 to 4	61	"	13·0	"	13·0

23. Comparative sickness of Goalpara and Gohatti.

The following valuable Table taken from Captain Pemberton's Report, will shew the comparative healthiness of the Eastern Frontier.

TABLE 4.

Statement of the Strength of Troops on the Eastern Frontier, the proportion of Sick and ratio per cent. of Deaths to Strength, for the years 1833, 1834 *and* 1835.

	DACCA.						JUMAULPORE.						SYLHET.						GOWAHATTY.						BISNAUTH.					
	Corps.	Average strength per annum.	Total admissions per annum.	Transferred.	Deaths.	Ratio per cent. of deaths to strength.	Corps.	Average strength per annum.	Total admissions per annum.	Transferred.	Deaths.	Ratio per cent. of deaths to strength.	Corps.	Average strength per annum.	Total admissions per annum.	Transferred.	Deaths.	Ratio per cent. of deaths to strength.	Corps.	Average strength per annum.	Total admissions per annum.	Transferred.	Deaths.	Ratio per cent. of deaths to strength.	Corps.	Average strength per annum.	Total admissions per annum.	Transferred.	Deaths.	Ratio per cent. of deaths to strength.
1833.	53 Regt. N. I.	743	310	1	10	1.34	35 Regt. N. I.	556	201	0	16	2.85	Sylhet L. I.	938	836	4	17	1.81	Dett. 35 Regt. N. I. for the month of June.	187	8	0	0	0	Assam L. I.	1129	686	7	14	1.25
1834.	53 Regt. N. I. relieved by 50 Regt. N. I. in Dec. 1834.	754	597	18	11	1.46	35 Regt. N. I.	582	427	6	6	1.3	Sylhet L. I.	940	875	4	11	1.16	Dett. Assam L. I. for 6 months	197	67	0	1	0.50	Assam L. I.	1129	759	25	28	2.48
*1835.	50 Regt. N. I.	587	507	34	9	1.53	58 Regt. N. I.	669	442	0	3	0 45	Sylhet L. I	941	1221	5	24	2.55	Dett. Assam Lt. Infy.	176	126	7	5	3	Assam L. I.	1093	464	11	8	0.73
	CHITTAGONG.						AKYAB.						KYOUK PHYOO.						SANDOWAY.											
1833.	11 Regt. N. I.	716	566	10	15	2.4	Dett. 25 Rt. N. I.	133	406	0	12	9	25 Rt. N. I.	255	651	0	21	8.40	Dett. 25 Regt. N. I. for 11 months.	149	126	3	7	4 68						
1834.	11 Regt. N. I.	704	574	14	17	2.42	Dett. 25 Rt. N. I. for 3 ms.	113	50	0	1	0.95	25 Rt. N. I.	386	735	14	11	2,90	Dett. 25 N. I. for 4 months.	119	29	0	1	0 84						
1835.	55 Regt. N. I.	601	490	0	29	4.83	....	....	....	..	..	....	40 Rt. N. I.	559	952	4	37	6.60	Dett. 40 Regt. N. I. for May.	167	7	0	0	0						

* For the year 1835, the averages only extend from January to September.

I am indebted to James Hutchinson, Esq., Secretary to the Medical Board, for this most valuable document, which satisfactorily shews the comparative salubrity of the different stations on the Eastern Frontier, and the extent to which mortality may be anticipated under ordinary circumstances.

CHAPTER XIII.

1, Revenue, Judicial and Police. 2, Feudal system. 3, Revenue system of Kamroop. 4, Revenue Officers. 5, Fees of Revenue Officers. 6, Private Estates how assessed. 7, House Tax. 8, Land Tax. 9, Abolition of Capitation and House Taxes. 10, Civil Courts. 11, Criminal Courts. 12, Police. 13. Omlahs Bengali. 14, Language of Courts. 15, Public Crime. 16, Punishment. 17, Insufficiency of Punishment. 18, Area of Kamroop. 19, Classes of Land. 20, Land Measure. 21, Population. 22, Stock. 23, Revenue and Disbursements. 24, Crime committed. 25, People killed by wild animals. 26, Population of Assam. 27, Receipts and Disbursements of Assam.

XIII.

1. Revenue, Judicial and Police.

The present Chapter I shall devote to the Revenue, Judicial and Police Departments. For the information contained in it, I am particularly indebted to the valuable papers of Captain Bogle's and Captain Matthie's, obligingly lent me by R. D. Mangles, Esq. Secretary to Government. As the mode of assessment used by the ancient Assamese Government is with but little modification practised at the present day, and as it exhibits anomalies very different from what prevails throughout India generally, I hope to be forgiven for entering somewhat into detail.

2. Feudal System.

It was one of the laws of the Assam Government, that the land and the subject were

XIII. equally the property of the State, and accordingly not only the houses and the lands, but the cultivators also were assessed. These were called *Pykes* or Serfs, and divided into squads of 3 or 4 called a *Gote*, each *Gote*, according to its calling or employment, was liable to be called upon to supply one of its *Pykes* to work for the good of the State. Hence the farmers, the fishermen, the boat builders, the oil-makers, the silk weavers, the tinkers, and the gold gatherers, all contributed their share to the Royal household, and filled it with the fat of the land. These Pykes had their Officers over hundreds and Officers over thousands; and the whole Serf population were under as rigid discipline as a regular army, and were obliged to take the field every man of the Gote, if called on to do so.

From an arrangement of this nature alone could the enormous public works, the tanks and bunds throughout Assam, have been effected: for the Pyke on duty cost the Government nothing, the other *Pykes* of his *Gote* contributed every thing for his subsistence, and the Sovereign had only to point out the work to be done. As a remuneration for these services each *Pyke* was allowed 3 pooras of land rent-free for cultivation, and in the event of their services not being required, each *Pyke* was liable to a poll tax of 2 or 3 rupees. This Pyke system was for some time continued by our Government, but from its not being found to answer well, it is now obsolete. It would be foreign to this paper to enumerate all the peculiarities of the ancient Assam Revenue system, but I believe I shall be able to give a more explicit account of the mode of collecting the Revenue of the present time, by detailing that in use in some particular Zillah, and for that purpsoe I shall select Kamroop. XIII.

3. Revenue System of Kamroop.

The Zillah of Kamroop is divided into 54 Pergunnahs, 5 Deshes, 9 Dwars and 7 Choumooas, and these when large are subdivided into Talooks and Mouzahs, with a still further distinction into Kiraj and Lakiraj Lands; Kiraj being applied to lands assessed to full amount, and Lakiraj to privileged lands which are assessed at a low rate.

4. Revenue Officers.

Each Mouzah or Village or Farm as it may be, has a headman called a Takooreea, or Mundul or Patgheri, who, with the assistance of a writer called a Gong-ka-goti, collects the Revenue of the Mouzah and pays it over to the Chowdrie, his immediate superior. The Chowdrie commonly extends his sway over five or more Mouzahs called a Talook, and is assisted by a Putwari, who keeps the account of the Pergunnah, and renders a statement to the Collector. The Revenue of Talooks generally average about 500 rupees per annum.

5. Fees of Revenue Officers.

These Officers receive a per-centage upon the amount of their collections as follows:

Chowdrie gets	7 per cent.	Takoorea gets	4 per cent.
Putwari „	1 „	Gong-ka-goti „	2½ „

XIII. Besides this they receive rent free land to the following amount on every 100 rupees of Collection :

Chowdrie gets	1 poora.		Takoorea gets	6 pooras.	
Putwari	„	½ „	Gong-ka-goti „	4	„

These petty Officers are allowed a certain number of peons, each of whom is entitled to a certain portion of rent free land or Maun-muttee, as it is called.

6. Private Estates how assessed.

Heritable proprietors with an income of more than 200 Rupees per annum, appoint their own Chowdries if they please, who pay the assessment into the Collectors ; those with less than 50 Rupees of annual income pay into Chowdries of Talook. Shuster's land or land set apart for religious or charitable purposes, of which kinds there are from 6 to 10 portions in each pergunnah, are assessed by the Shusters Burwa, who pays the amount direct into the Collector. In like manner all the Temple lands have each its own manager, who pays the Revenue into the Collector not into Chowdrie.

7. House Tax.

Until lately the Revenue was raised chiefly by taxes upon houses and lands. Each house or family paid a tax more or less according to their means. The number of families instead of being calculated according to the number of hearths, was estimated by the number of Churoos or family plates so called, each family possessing one from which they all eat ; so that the number of families was most correctly known from the Churoos ; every family was taxed according to its wealth, and the plan in use to ascertain that was to number their ploughs. Hence, a XIII.

family with	3 Ploughs paid	3 Rs.	per annum.
,,	2 ,,	2	,,
,,	1 ,,	1	,,
,,	without a plough	12 As.	,,

This rate was equal in Kiraj and Lakiraj lands.

The next source of Revenue was the land-tax. 8. Land Tax.

This was generally determined by measure ment, each poorah of land being assessed according to its quality.

	Kiraj Lands.			*Lakiraj Lands.*
Roopeet Land,	1st class paid	1 Rs.	}	4 As. per poora.
,,	2d ,,	12		
Bautullie,	1st ,,	12	}	2 ,,
,,	2d ,,	8		
Furringuttee,	1st ,,	8	}	1 ,, 6½ ,,
,,	2d ,,	4		

Many pieces of land did not admit of measurement such as sand-banks, islands, &c. constantly changing, and with only spots here and there fit for cultivation. These were assessed by the number of ploughs; the ryot paying Rs. 2-8 for as much as he could cultivate with each plough. .

Though the house tax of the Kiraj and the Lakiraj were the same, the land tax as seen above is so trivial on the latter as to be merely nominal.

Very lately the capitation and the house taxes were abolished throughout Assam, and to meet the deficiency of Revenue the taxes on 9. Abolition of Capitation and House Taxes.

XIII. lands were increased in the following proportions: in addition to the rate above stated.

Bāri Lands, ...	Rs.	1	per poora.
Bāri ditto, ...	As.	4	„
Roopeet ditto, ...	„	4	„
Bautullie ditto, ...	„	4	„
Furrunguttee ditto, ...	„	2	„

The Judicial and Police Departments as well as the Revenue, are all three performed by the Senior Assistant to the Agent of the Governor General or Commissioner.

10. Civil Courts. 1. All Suits above 1,000 rupees are cognizable by the Commissioner's Court alone, as well as all Appeals from decisions of the Senior Assistant's Court.

2. All Suits between 500 and 1,000 rupees are decided by the Senior Assistant, as also Appeals from the inferior Native Courts.

3. All Suits between 100 and 500 rupees are decided by the Sudder Moonsiff's Court, who hears Appeals from the Moonsiff's Punchaet.

4. All Suits under 100 rupees are decided by the Moonsiff's Punchaet.

11. Criminal Courts. The Senior Assistant, aided by a Jury, investigates all crimes of a heinous nature, and submits the case for confirmation to the Commissioner.

The Police is managed by Darogahs, Thannadars and Peons stationed thoughout the District, assisted by the Takoorias or Patgeris and Chowdries of the Revenue Department. XIII. 12. Police.

The greater number of the Native Establishments is composed of Bengalis, the Assamese form but a small share, being found less fitted for office and only a few being qualified. 13. Omlahs Bengali

The language in general use is Bengali, all the business of the Courts is written in that character with the exception of some Roobakaris, which are written in Persian. 14. Language of Courts.

Public crime generally speaking is very much on the decrease, murder is very rare, and burglary, cattle stealing and petty thefts are the most common as will be seen from Tables. Nine-tenths of the complaints in the Civil Courts are frivolous, and many of them false, or done in the spirit of annoying the defender. 15. Public Crime.

Fine and imprisonment are the only punishments, now that corporal punishment has been abolished; but few are able to pay a fine, and most who can pay prefer imprisonment to loss of money. The old system of the ratan is now much wanted, the guilty individual was by a few stripes made sensible of his misdemeanour, the example it shewed was much more striking and its impressions were not soon forgotten, and none but the offender was a sufferer. In comparison to ratanning, the present system of 16. Punishment.

XIII. imprisonment has no terrors to the guilty, he knows if he is imprisoned he shall have a home and a subsistence ; if he is not troubled with a moderate share of shame, he may contrive to live not so bad a life after all. But the evils of the present system do not rest with the offender ; if he has a family depending upon him for food and clothing, they too are made to suffer for the crime of the father, by being left destitute, and the misery thus entailed can be readily imagined.

17. Insufficiency of Punishment. The want of corporal punishment is no less felt amongst the Seapoys of the Provincial Battalions than amongst the prisoners. Few of them are gifted with much *esprit de corps*, their principal, often their sole, object in joining the regiment is to serve four or five years, and save a few rupees to enable them to establish themselves in petty farming: a court martial can have but little terror for them, and its severest sentence of dismissal from the Service is at worst only a disappointment, and not unfrequently a desirable release from their engagement.

I believe I am correct in asserting that both the Civil and Military authorities in Assam, feel their efficiency impaired from not being able to avail themselves of the salutary influence of the ratan.

Kamroop is divided into Kamroop north of the Brahmaputra, Kamroop south of the Brahmaputra and the Islands of the River. The following Tables shew the Area in Assam Pooras, the different kinds of Land, and Land Measure, Population, Stock, Revenue and Disbursement for 1834-5.

18—AREA OF KAMROOP.

	Rice cultivation.	Booree Land.	Village Land.	Uncultivated Land.	Total.	Remarks.
N. Kamroop,	211437¼	48177¾	62429	531962¼	854006¼	The River includes the site of town Gohatti.
S. Kamroop,	71563¼	10710¼	12755½	312452½	407482½	
River	......	......	......	72015	72015	
	283000½	58888	75184½	916429¾	1333503¾	

About $\frac{1}{10}$ of Country is Village and Plantation Lands.

$\frac{2}{10}$ Under Rice Cultivation.

$\frac{7}{10}$ Waste as Jungles, Hills, Rivers.

19—CLASSES OF LAND.

	1st Class or Roopeet.				2d Class or Bautullie.				3d Class or Furringutti.				Total Cultivation.			
Kiraj, ..	101135	0	0	12	20973	3	0	3	30508	1	3	3	152617	0	3	18
Lakiraj,	6763	3	3	12	12051	2	0	8	12946	3	4	12	92636	1	3	12
	107898	3	4	4	33025	5	0	11	43455	1	2	15	245253	2	2	10

20—LAND MEASURE.

1 Tar Square,	=	1 Leesa.	5 Khatas,	=	1 Doon.
20 Leesas,	=	1 Khata.	4 Doons,	=	1 Poora.

A Poora is equal to 3⅓ Bigas, equal to about 1⅓ Acre.

21—POPULATION.

	Churoos.	Adult Men.	Adult Women.	Boys.	Girls.	Slaves and Bondsmen.	Slaves and Bondswomen.	Total of Souls.
Kiraj, ...	35941	51211	42704	22403	13098	5793	4161	139370
Lakiraj, ...	29174	39069	30724	15807	8250	5810	4287	103947
Grand Total.	65115	90280	73428	38210	21348	11603	8448	243317

Probably 300000 is nearer the population than the number stated; of these there may be—

Mahomedans, ... 20000

Hindoos, ... 280000

22—STOCK.

	Ploughs.	Plough Cattle.	Cows and Heifers.	Buffaloes.	Total Horned Cattle.	Remarks.
Kiraj,	30031½	60063	78408	422	138893	
Lakiraj,	16084	32168	49175	434	81777	
Total..	46115½	92231	127583	856	220670	

23—REVENUE AND DISBURSEMENT.

Gross Revenue, ...	0	0	0	0	213348	4	15	3
Add Ferry Fund, ...	0	0	0	0	1006	0	0	0
Bootan Tribute, ...	0	0	0	0	2937	12	6	2
					217292	1	5	5
Mofussil Charges, ...	31751	10	13	1				
Annual Sudder ditto.	80400	0	0	0				
					112151	10	13	1
Balance saved.					105140	6	8	0

24.

Comparative Statement of Crimes of a heinous nature ascertained by the Police Officers or otherwise, within the District of Kamroop, for 1833 *and* 1834.

Zillah, ..	Year.	Decoity.	Highway Robbery.	Burglary.	Cattle Stealing.	Theft.	Affray.	Wilful Murder.	Homicide.	Receiving Stolen Property.	Arson.	Rape.	Adultery.	Perjury.	Forgery.
Kamroop,	1833	20	2	289	134	126	9	0	9	0	5	4	1	3	6
	1834	17	1	120	22	120	6	0	5	0	4	2	1	2	2

25.

Statement of the number of persons known to have been killed by wild Animals within the District of Durrung, during 1833 *and* 1834.

Year.	By wild Elephants.	By wild Buffaloes.	By Tigers.	By wild Hogs.	By Alligators.	Total.
1833	17	2	4	2	0	25
1834	17	0	8	1	1	27
				Grand Total.....		52

26—POPULATION OF ASSAM.

Districts.		
Assam Rajah, ...	....	220000
Durrung, ...	....	89519
Nowgong, ...	....	90000
Kamroop, ...	....	300000
Goalpara, ...	Not ascertained but probably,	100000
	Grand Total. ..	799519

27—*Abstract of Revenue and Charges of Assam, Goalparah, and Northern Jynteeah as per Capt. Pemberton's Report.*

RECEIPTS.	Cos. Rs. As. Ps.	Cos. Rs. As. Ps.
Land Revenue.		
Kamroop, .. } ..... Assam, { ....(estimated,)	2,00,000 0 0	
Durrung, .. } Assam, { .... ditto	1,00,000 0 0	
Nowgong, .. } ..... Assam, { .... ditto	60,000 0 0	
Zillah Goalparah, including Cooch Behar,	81,844 4 6	
		4,41,844 4 6
Add.		
Garrow Haut collections at Goalparah ..	41,500 0 0	
Rent of Garrow Mehauls and Garrow Nuzzuranna, about..............	4,000 0 0	
Sale of Opium at Goalparah,..........	14,200 0 0	
Abkarry Collections, ...	3,322 0 0	
Sale of Stamps, ...	7,303 5 0	
		70,325 5 0
Upper Assam Tribute,................	50,000 0 0	
Jynteeah estimated Revenue,..........	5,000 0 0	
		55,000 0 0
		5,67,169 9 6
Deduct Civil Establishments and other charges, as per annexed statement, ..	....	5,42,789 3 11
	Diff. Compy.'s Rupees	24,380 5 7

The Customs, amounting to Sicca Rupees 21,124 14 17 have been discontinued, and are not included in the Estimate of Goalparah Revenue.
F J.

DISBURSEMENTS.	Cos. Rs. As. Ps per month.	Cos. Rs. As. Ps.	Cos. Rs. As Ps. per annum.
General Charges.			
Agent's Establishment, including Agent's Salary, per mensem, ...	3,010 0 0		
Agent's Establishment, travelling allowances, ...	607 7 5		
„ Contingency, ...	500 0 0		
Commissioner's Office, ...	835 0 0		
„ Judicial Contingency,	160 2 4		
„ Revenue Contingency,	153 9 10	for 12 months is,	63,194 11 0
	5,266 3 7		
Political Agent, Upper Assam and Suddya, ...	1,843 7 6½	„ „	22,121 10 8
Assam Light Infantry,......	12,719 13 10	„ „	1,52,648 6 0
„ Sebundy Corps, ...	5,500 0 0	„ „	66,000 0 0
		Compy.'s Rs.	3,03,064 11 8
Civil Establishment.			
Kamroop, ...	4,874 0 0	for 12 months is, 58,488 0 0	
Durrung, ...	2,926 12 0	35,121 0 0	
Nowgong, ...	2,704 0 0	32,448 0 0	
Goalparah, ...	6,813 15 4	81,767 8 3	
			2,07,824 8 3
			5,11,789 3 11
Revenue Survey Department,............			7,000 0 0
			5,18,789 3 11
Add for Contingencies of the four Divisions, ... }	(uncertain) 2000	per month,....	24,000 0 0
		Company's Rupees	5,42,789 3 11

(Signed) F. JENKINS.

CHAPTER XIV.

HILL TRIBES OF ASSAM.

1, *Booteas*. 2, *Akas*. 3, *Duphlas*. 4, *Koppachors*. 5, *Miris*. 6, *Abors*. 7, *Bor-Abors*. 8, *Mishmis*. 9, *Kangtis*. 10, *Bor-Kangtis*. 11, *Singphos*. 12, *Mattucks*. 13, *Nagas*. 14, *Muniporis*. 15, *Cacharis*. 16, *Kassyas*. 17, *Garrows*. 18, *Rabas*. 19, *Lalungs*. 20, *Chooteas*. 21, *Mikirs*.

XIV. HILL TRIBES.

As the very numerous hill tribes that surround Assam, occupy a prominent place in the statistics of the province, either from their contributing largely to the population and tillage of the valley, from the trade they maintain with the Assamese, the hostile incursions they still occasionally make upon their unsuspecting neighbours, the treaties of tribute or alliance that unite their interests with Government, the stern neutrality of their policy towards strangers or the determined resistance to all ingress into the interior of their country, I shall endeavour to give a brief outline of the relative position of each in its respective order.

I am afraid, that what I have previously written, may be thought somewhat too elaborate; but, my excuse is, that it is the topography not of a single Zillah, but of a whole kingdom; and to provide against any charges of prolixity

XIV. HILL TRIBES.

in this division I hope I need only premise the number of states that compose it, each of which might be made the subject of a separate paper.

Few nations bordering upon the British dominions in India are less generally known than those inhabiting the extreme N. E. Frontier of Bengal; and yet, in a commercial, a statistical, or a political point of view, no country is more important. There our territory of Assam is situated in almost immediate contact with the empires of China and Ava, being separated from each by a narrow belt of mountainous country, possessed by barbarous tribes of independent savages, and capable of being crossed over in the present state of communication in 10 or 12 days. From this mountain range, navigable branches of the great rivers of Nankin, of Cambodia, of Martaban, of Ava, and of Assam derive their origin, and appear designed by nature as the great highways of commerce between the nations of Ultra Gangetic Asia. In that quarter, our formidable neighbours, the Burmese, have been accustomed to make their inroads into Assam; there, in the event of hostilities, they are certain to attempt it again; and there, in case of its ever becoming necessary to take vengeance on the Chinese, an armed force embarking on the Brahmaputra, could be speedily marched across the intervening country to the banks of the greatest rivers of China, which would conduct them through the very centre of the celestial empire to the ocean.

This beautiful tract of country, though thinly populated by straggling hordes of barbarians, and allowed to lie profitless in impenetrable jungle, enjoys all the qualities requisite for rendering it one of the finest in the world. Its climate is cold, healthy, and congenial to European constitutions; its numerous crystal streams abound in gold dust, and masses of the solid metal; its mountains are pregnant with precious stones and silver; its atmosphere is perfumed with tea growing wild and luxuriantly; and its soil is so well adapted to all kinds of agricultural purposes, that it might be converted into one continued garden of silk, and cotton, and coffee, and sugar, and tea, over an extent of many hundred miles.

XIV. HILL TRIBES.

The Hill Tribes of Assam may be divided into two grand divisions, those on the north of Assam, viz. the Booteas, Akas, Duphlas, Koppachors, Miris, Abors, Bor Abors, Mishmis, Kangtis, and Bor Kangtis; and those on the south in continuation of the circuit, viz. the Singphos, Mattucks, Nagas, Munniporis, Cacharis, Kassyas, and Garrows.

Of all these the Booteas are the most important, and as they are the first in this arrangement, I shall commence with them.

Section I.—Booteas.

1, *Boundaries and Extent.* 2, *Cultivation.* 3, *Dwars.* 4, *Tribute to Honorable Company.* 5, *Government, Dhurm Rajah.* 6, *Daeb Rajah.* 7, *Capitals.* 8, *Revenue and Pay of Public Officers.* 9, *People.* 10, *Army.* 11, *Religion.* 12, *Anomalous Marriages.* 13, *Trade.*

XIV. HILL TRIBES. 1. Boundaries and Extent. Boot or Bhot, is a term generally applicable to that middle ground that lies between the great Himalya range and the plains, and the inhabitants are known by the name of Bhoots or Booteas; but the term Bootan is confined to that hilly country, the centre of which is due north of Goalpara. Bootan is bounded on the west by the Sikim country, on the north by Thibet, on the east by the Akas, and on the south by Assam. Its length from west to east is about twenty-two days' journey, and breadth from north to south from ten to fifteen.

2. Cultivation. Though a cold mountainous rugged country, it is in a forward state of cultivation; there is but very little level land in the interior, but the brows of the hills are cut out into terraces, the one rising above the other, and irrigated by numerous mountain streams. The mountains towards the plains rise so very perpendicularly that there are but comparatively few places where an entrance on foot or on horseback can be effected; the chief of these I have already mentioned in Chap. I., para. 12. The roads

are not adapted for any kind of carriage, and the conveyance of the country is either on the shoulders or ponies. XIV. HILL TRIBES.

3. Dwars.

The territory of Bootan is properly confined within the hills; but, during the ancient Assam Government, certain lands in the plains were from political reasons allotted them for the cultivation of rice, for which their hills were not adapted. These lands were called dwars, and to guard against the Booteas claiming them in perpetuity, they were allowed to keep possession and act as sovereigns only during eight months of the year (the season of cropping); while they reverted to the Assam Government during the other four months. This constant change of jurisdiction afforded a favourable resort for all the vagabonds of both countries, and these dwars long continued the head quarters of gangs of robbers and other delinquents, who made incursions either into the hills or the plains as it suited their convenience. These dwars, besides contributing greatly to the sustenance of the Booteas, also yield a considerable revenue to the Bootan Government. They are rented by some of the officers of state, who pay tribute amounting to about forty thousand rupees yearly.

4. Tribute to Honourable Company.

A small tribute, merely nominal, was exacted from the Booteas on account of these dwars, consisting of—

24 Tolahs Gold Dust,
30 Ponies,

XIV. HILL TRIBES.

24 Bags of Musk,
24 Yaks' Tails,
24 Blankets,
24 Daggers,

valued in toto about 30,000 rupees. On our Government assuming the sovereignty of Assam, the same privilege on the same conditions was granted to them, and still continues unaltered. But the value of these articles has of late years been very much deteriorated; the ponies they send are the lame, the blind, the vicious and diseased; the musk is generally largely adulterated with dried blood; the blanket are mere ribbons about nine inches broad and coarse as gunny bags; and the daggers have nothing of a dagger but the name.

5. Government Dhurm Rajah.

The Government of Bootan is vested in the Dhurm Rajah and the Daeb Rajah. The Dhurm Rajah does not condescend to trouble himself with worldly matters, but devotes his time and attention entirely to religious concerns. At the same time that he is considered the real Sovereign of the people, he is looked up to as their spiritual guide and even worshipped as a god. The Dhurm Rajah is believed never to die, but when the corporeal frame of his temporary abode has been worn out and committed to the dust, the etherial essence takes possession of some newly created body, and is found regenerated in some infant child.

6. Daeb Rajah.

The Daeb Rajah, though subservient to the Dhurm, and only holding the office of Prime Minister, may be called the actual Sovereign.

XIV. HILL TRIBES.

On him devolves all transactions with foreign Governments as well as the internal affairs of state. The office is not hereditary, for any individual may rise to the dignity; neither is it an appointment for life, but only for a series of years. He may resign office if he thinks proper, and that period is frequently cut short by some alleged mismanagement or the intrigue of opposing parties. Eight chief officers of state sit in council with the Daeb Rajah, without whose concurrence he cannot proceed. 100 Zinkaubs or Zinkaffs attend upon the Daeb Rajah in readiness to dispatch upon any business of the Government.

7. Capitals.

Tassisudon is considered the capital of Bootan, but the Court only reside there during the hottest weather. In the winter season it is deserted on account of the intense cold, and Dosen or Punaka becomes the seat of Government. This emigration is common with many of the inhabitants, who cultivate one farm in the mountains in summer, and another in the lower lands in winter.

8. Revenue and Pay of Public Officers.

The whole revenue of Bootan does not amount to much more than three lacks of rupees. The country is farmed out in Rajhships, the holder being some officer of state who pays a certain sum in cash yearly. All public officers are paid in produce from the public stores, a mere subsistence; and such as no public officer would be contented with unless some perquisites or privileges were attached to office. But extortion is a great source of income to

XIV. HILL TRIBES.

Government servants in Bootan, besides they monopolize all the trade of the country, for none but they are allowed to trade with a foreign country. Even the Dhurm and the Daeb Rajahs have large capitals invested in trade.

9. People.

The Booteas are a middle or rather undersized race of men, more remarkable for tension of sinew than weight of limb; their features are purely Tartar; their dress consists of a tunic of coarsest cotton or woolen cloth, secured by a waist belt and coming down below the knees. In general they wear no tail, but have their hair hanging loose about their ears, or wound round their heads in a fold of cotton ; however I have seen some wearing their hair in the Chinese fashion. Their persons are extremely filthy, and there is an air of meanness and poverty about those holding offices of considerable trust and importance, betokening a very poor pittance allowed for their services ; they are acknowledged to be a very quiet, industrious and civilized race ; many of their laws and customs they have copied from the Chinese. The Chinese themselves are not more guarded against the visitation of foreigners, and in any attempts to enter their country, they are instantly opposed by parties in charge of the dwars or passes, who are proof against either recompense or entreaty.

10. Army.

No race have less genius for war than the Booteas, the petty feuds that frequently break out amongst themselves only excite our ridicule ; their grand tactic is ambuscade, and unless they can take their enemy at a disadvantage they very rarely join in open combat. Yet their soldiers go well cased in iron helmets and chain armour or mail; they carry matchlocks which they are afraid (and not without reason) to fire; and lots of knives and bows and arrows. The people go armed at all times, and even the women wear knives for their protection.

XIV. HILL TRIBES.

In the field every man provides his own subsistence. The Bootea soldiers are held in the utmost contempt by our Seapoys. On a late occasion a skirmish took place on the frontier between about 700 Booteas and 70 men of the Assam Sebundy Corps, when the former were, after the second volley, driven in consternation to their hills, with the loss of upwards of 25 men. The Sebundies had not a man wounded.

11. Religion.

The religion of Bootan is Buddhism, their priests are called Gelums who live in Monkish celibacy. They are very numerous and form a large proportion of the populace. To them is intrusted the funeral rites of the people. Public places for the incineration of the dead are built, the Gelums attend the ceremony; when the body is reduced to ashes, the ashes are put into a brass vessel and carried in procession to some river into which they are thrown, and the Gelum claims the vessel as his perquisite. Convents are not unfrequent in Bootan.

12. Anomalous Marriages.

Prostitution is very common; most of the women, it is reported, spend their earliest years

XIV. HILL TRIBES. in that condition, and it is no uncommon thing for two or three brothers to club together and share one woman between them. The eldest brother is considered the father of what offspring may take place, and the younger as uncles.

13. Trade. The trade with Bootan is at present very inconsiderable, not so much from there being no scope, as from the exclusive privilege of its government and servants to trade; and the prohibition of private individuals. Horses are the principal export, but no mares are allowed to go out of the country. If a European Resident were established at the Capital and this monopoly abolished, there is reason to believe that a very important trade might be established with Bootan. English merchants could far undersell them in woolens and coarse cottons, and in return might get large quantities of musk and Cashmere wool; the musk deer, and the shawl goat being indigenous. Barter is the most general mode of trading in Bootan. When the government are hard pressed for money they frequently dispatch a messenger to one of the stations in the plains with some article of value. I remember a Zinkaff coming to Goalpara, bringing two wretched ponies with him and offering them to the Magistrate for so much pure gold as he should think them worth. The Dhurm Rajah had then lately died, and was found regenerated in a child. On installing him in office it is necessary to cover the palace with gold, and this was one of the plans adopted for raising the sum. On another occasion, a party arrived with a maund

of ivory, which they valued at 400 rupees; in exchange for this they demanded a musket with 8lbs. of gun-powder, to be valued at the discretion of the Magistrate, and the balance in cash; but I believe neither speculation answered their purpose. XIV. HILL TRIBES.

SECTION II.—AKAS, DUPHLAS, AND KOPPACHORS.

1, *Fierce People.* 2, *Levy Black Mail.*

Of these three tribes but little is known, more than that they are a warlike ferocious people, who make plunder their profession, and live in a good measure by levying black mail from the cultivators in the plains. But Government have lately commuted the black mail to an equivalent in cash paid out of the Public Treasury. Not long ago a party of Duphlas suddenly surprised a Havildar's guard of the Assam Light Infantry stationed on the Chardwar frontier, and cut almost every man, woman and child to pieces. 1. Fierce People. 2. Levy Black Mail.

SECTION III.—MIRIS.

1, *Extent.* 2, *Manners and Customs.* 3, *Eat Poisoned Animals.*

The Miris occupy that strip of alluvial land along the northern bank of the Brahmaputra, from the large island Majuli to the river Dihong, the northern branch of the Brahmaputra; and are bounded on the north by the hill country of the Abors. Till of late years, this district was deserted on account of the ravages of the 1. Extent.

XIV. HILL TRIBES. Abors; but on our affording them protection, the original inhabitants returned. The land is still very thinly populated, and the only cultivation is along the banks of the great river. Their head village is Motgong.

2. Manners and Customs. The manners and habits of the Miris are wild and barbarous, and their persons filthy and squalid; they use a language different from the Assamese, and make use of bows and poisoned arrows, as a defence against their enemies. They are expert marksmen; and the poison used is so fatal, that even a scratch of their arrow is followed with certain death. 3. Eat Poisoned Animals. They eat all sorts of wild animals, not excepting those killed by their own poisonous arrows. The Miris are an industrious race, and partial to living in the skirts of the forests, clearing new ground, which they cultivate for a year or two, and then moving off to another place, when the soil is exhausted. A great deal of opium is grown by the Miris, which they barter for grain with the Assamese.

SECTION IV.—ABORS, BOR-ABORS, AND MISHMIS.

1, *Extent.* 2, *Houses.* 3, *Hospitality.* 4, *Preserve Skulls of Cattle.* 5, *Migration.* 6, *Trade.*

1. Extent. These tribes inhabit an extensive range of mountainous country, along the southern exposure of the great Himalaya chain, from the 94th to the 97th degree of east longitude, and border with Thibet and China. It is difficult to form a conception of the extent of these tribes, but they are not to be despised; for during the insurrection of the Muamarias, no less than

17,000 Abors joined to drive that tribe out of Assam. It is probable that at no ancient period these two tribes were unconnected, but the Mishmis, are now considered by the Abors as dependent upon them, and treated as slaves. Besides the Mishmis here mentioned as subservient to the Abors, there are several tribes of them, such as Muzu-Mishmis and Taen-Mishmis inhabiting the extreme branches of the Lohit or eastern channel of the Brahmaputra, who are probably independent. These tribes possess one of the lowest grades of civilization, they occupy numerous villages along the precipitous shores of the two great northern branches of the Brahmaputra, the Dihong or Sampo, and the Dibong. XIV. HILL TRIBES.

2. Houses.

Their houses are so constructed that the perpendicular side of the rock forms one wall: the floor is made of bambus, with one side supported on the rock, and the other on beams driven into the ground. The space underneath is inhabited by the cattle, and the interstices in the floor afford the double advantage of showering down all the offal to the herd below, and preventing the accumulation of filth and nastiness.

3. Hospitality

Though the snows of their mountain home have narrowed their means of subsistence, and limited their intercourse to their immediate neighbours, yet they are a hospitable and even a social race; and a constant round of festivity is kept up from one end of the year to the other. Each chieftain kills the fatted bullock in turn; all his associates are invited to par-

XIV. HILL TRIBES.

take of the good cheer: the host is in his turn a guest at the next feast; and thus a reciprocity of entertainment is insured.

4. Preserve Skulls of Cattle.

Nor are these hospitable rites allowed to be forgotten; the skull of every animal that has graced the board, is hung up as a record in the hall of the entertainer; he who has the best stocked Golgotha, is looked upon as the man of the greatest wealth and liberality; and when he dies, the whole smoke-dried collection of many years is piled upon his grave, as a monument of his riches, and a memorial of his worth.

5. Migration.

These people, accustomed to a temperature at and about the freezing point, seem to dread an exposure to the heat of the low countries during the summer, and make their descent to their markets at Suddia only in the cold weather, and take their departure to their snows as soon the Simala tree puts forth its blossoms.

6. Trade.

They bring along with them a few bags of musk, and musk deer skins; some ivory, a few copper pots, which they obtain from the Lama country; and a considerable quantity of a vegetable poison called Bisa, used in poisoning arrows. These they exchange for glass beads, of which they are very fond; and cattle, for the purpose of eating. The musk is for the most part adulterated; a portion of the genuine musk being abstracted to make into artificial bags, and its place filled up with dried blood.

SECTION V.—KANGTIS.

XIV. HILL TRIBES.

1, *Extent.* 2, *Descent.* 3, *Superiority.* 4, *Suddia.* 5, *Force.*

1. Extent.

The Kangtis are the most civilized of all these mountain tribes; they inhabit that triangular tract of country bounded by the Lohit on the one side, by the Dihong on the other, and by the mountainous country belonging to the Mishmis on the third.

2. Descent.

They are descended from the Bor Kangtis, a powerful race, situated on the sources of the Irrawaddi. About fifty or sixty years ago, they emigrated from their native country, and availing themselves of the civil war then raging throughout Assam, took forcible possession of the country they now enjoy, ejected the reigning Chieftain; the Suddia Cowa Gohaing; and the Kangti Chief, usurping his name and jurisdiction, reduced his subjects to dependence or slavery.

3. Superiority.

The Kangtis, by a vigorous mode of government, and holding out an asylum to refugees from other states, soon rose to eminence. They are now a superior race to all their neighbours; they are tall, fair, and handsome, considerably advanced in civilization, and are endowed with no small share of military courage. Their religion is Buddhism; but Hinduism is gaining progress. They are amongst the few tribes who have a written character, and can read and write the Burmese language, and understand it when spoken. Their own language, though written, and in

XIV. HILL TRIBES. character a good deal resembling the Burmese, is quite different, and closely resembles the original Ahom. Every boy is taught to read and write it by the priests.

Suddia is the capital of the Kangti country, and the Chieftain is known by the name of the Suddia Cowa Gohaing, and claims descent from the Royal family of Assam. The Suddia Cowa Gohaing is believed to be a firm friend of Chandra Kant's, the ex-rajah of Assam; when formerly driven from the kingdom, the Suddia Cowa had influence enough at the Court of Ava to obtain the assistance of the Burmese to restore him to his throne.

4. Suddia. Suddia is situated on the right bank of the Kunil or Kundil nallah, and about six miles above its junction with the Lohit. It is a place of some importance, and has a population of about 4000 men, exclusive of women and children. Its trade is rapidly increasing; all the necessaries of life are procurable: its exports are gold and silver, amber, musk, and ivory; Kangti daus, Chinese and Burmese trinkets; Bisa-poison, and dye-stuffs, called Mishmi-tita, and manjit. The Mishmi-tita, manjit, and lime, triturated with water, and allowed to digest in an earthen pot for a month, makes a beautiful permanent red dye. The daus are of a high order, and are so much prized as to bring 12 rupees a piece. They are manufactured by a rude wild race, called Kunungs, (slaves to the Kangtis,) who are situated on the

extreme branches of the Irrawaddi, who can neither read nor write. XIV. HILL TRIBES.

The country around Suddia is composed of the richest alluvial soil, well adapted for cultivation, but is generally flat and liable to inundation. A large portion of it is waste, and overgrown with jungle: it is closely surrounded by the snowy mountains, which are only about thirty or forty miles distant; and the water of the river is so cold, that of itself it serves to cool wine for table.

Suddia is the most advanced post we possess on the north-east frontier. Four companies of the Assam Light Infantry are stationed there, under the command of a European Officer, invested with political authority. Two gun-boats are also stationed there, under the command of a European—each boat has one 12-pounder mounted on slides, and is well manned and equipped for service: one of the boats is manned by Kangtis, who give much satisfaction. There is also a small stockade erected, with a few guns mounted. Suddia has hitherto preserved a healthy character. The Suddia Cowa Gohaing, though he pays Government no tribute, acknowledges the Company's supremacy, and is bound to furnish a contingent of 200 men. That contingent is supplied by arms and ammunition at the expense of Government; they are drilled by the Subadar of the Assam Light Infantry four months in the year, and the arms, when in want of repair, are forwarded to head-quarters at Bishnath. No 5. Force.

XIV. HILL TRIBES.

Medical Officer is attached to Suddia. An Apothecary is entrusted with Medical charge.

Section VI.—Bor-Kangtis.

1, Subjects of Ava. 2, Silver Mine. 3, Munglung Kangtis.

1. Subjects of Ava.

The Bor-Kangtis are a numerous and powerful race, situated amongst the mountains whence the Irrawaddi takes it origin. They are under the Government of Ava, and supply a contingency to the Burmese army. Experienced Burmese Officers are constantly traversing their country for the purpose of drilling them, and inspecting their arms and ammunition. The capital of the Bor-Kangtis is Manchi, on a remote branch of the Irrawaddi: this place was visited by Lieutenants Wilcox and Burlton in 1827, by an overland route, across the mountains from Suddia. The journey occupied about 12 days: they were kindly received by the Bor-Kangti chief, who gave them every information about the sources of the Irrawaddi, and convinced them that from the smallness of the streams, it was impossible for any of them to afford a channel for the waters of the Sampu. The main stream of the Irrawaddi is there fordable, and not more than eighty yards broad.

2. Silver Mine.

There is a silver mine in the Bor-Kangti country; but it has never produced more than 8,000 rupees a year. It might be turned to much more advantage; but the possessors are afraid of increasing its revenue, lest by doing so they should excite the avarice of their neighbours. There are also mines of lead and iron in this country.

We have lately come into intimate contact with another tribe of Kangtis called Munglung; these, from dissension amongst themselves, and from the oppression of the Burmese, have lately dispatched about 200 of their tribe to stipulate for settlements in the British dominions, and report on the prospects of the country around Suddia. Should their report prove favourable, about 5,000 more have expressed their desire to emigrate.

SECTION VII.—SINGPHOS.

1, *Boundaries.* 2, *Chiefs.* 3, *Irruptions.* 4, *Wakum Koonjie's Invasion.* 5, *Bisa Gaum.* 6, *Duffa Gaum.* 7, *Caste.* 8, *Religion.* 9, *Language.* 10, *Marriages.* 11, *Funeral Rites.* 12, *Inheritance.* 13, *Intercourse with Burmese Singphos.*

By far the most powerful and the most formidable of these hill tribes are the Singphos; 1. Boundaries.
they are also the most numerous, and are scattered over the greatest extent of country. They are bounded on the north by the Lohit river, on the east by the Langtan mountains, which separate them from the Bor-Kangtis, on the south by the Patkoi range, which divides them from the Burmese Singphos, from whom they are descended, and on the west, by a line drawn south from Suddia, till it meets the last mentioned mountains.

XIV. HILL TRIBES. 2. Chiefs. The Singphos are divided into 12 principal tribes, each having its own Chief or Gaum; but every chieftain maintains his own separate independence, and seldom unites with any other, unless it be to punish some aspiring Chief obnoxious to them all, or in making plundering excursions upon neighbouring States.

All the Chiefs have claimed our protection, though no tribute is exacted from them; with one or two exceptions, they have acted up to their engagements.

3. Irruptions. The Singphos have, for several generations, been the terror of the wretched Assamese, and were in the constant habit of making irruptions into their country, sometimes as far as their very capital itself; of plundering their temples, laying waste their country, and carrying off the inhabitants into slavery. Since the British troops have had possession of Assam, these inroads have been prevented; but as might be expected, they are somewhat impatient of that restraint, and have once or twice endeavoured to resort to their old habits. To give an idea of the extent to which these devastations were carried on, the late Captain Neufville, received from the Singphos alone upwards of 7,000 Assamese captive slaves; and, perhaps, there are 100,000 Assamese and Manipuris still in slavery throughout the dominions of Ava.

4. Wakum Koonjie's Invasion. About five years ago, a body of them amounting to about 3,000 men, armed with spears, daus, and a few musquets and jinjals, under a

Chief called Wakum Koonjie, made an advance against the station of Suddia, with the confident intention of carrying away in chains every Seapoy present, and of driving the British out of the country. This wàs a plot of three years' concocting, large stores of grain were accumulated in convenient depots, and shackles for ten thousand prisoners were all in readiness; but the whole force was shamefully repulsed by the then Political Agent, Captain Neufville, at the head of a handful of men of the Assam Infantry, and a few armed Kangti and Muamaria Militia, and driven in consternation into their hills. The Lubona Gaum only, of all the 12 Chiefs, took part in this irruption, and has taken an active hand in the late disturbances, headed by the Duffa Gaum.

The Bisa Gaum or Chief is a man of superior understanding, and was entrusted by the late Agent to the Governor General, the lamented Mr. Scott, with a good deal of confidence, and had an allowance from Government of 50 Rupees a month, as an organ of communication with the other Chiefs. The late Captain Neufville was also confident of his integrity, and made proposals to him to desert his own country, to live on lands to be granted him at Borhath and Jaipur, and allow his native hills to become a wilderness, and form a natural barrier against the incursions of the other tribes. He furnishes a contingent of about 100 men, and is supplied with arms and ammunition. 5. Bisa Gaum.

The most influential of the unfriendly Chiefs is the Duffa Gaum. Only a few months ago 6. Duffa Gaum.

XIV. HILL TRIBES. he made a hostile incursion against our ally the Bisa Gaum, and massacred every man, woman, and child he could get near; the Bisa Gaum narrowly escaped with his life, and some of his own family were cut to pieces. After two or three skirmishes, the marauders were dislodged, and driven to their hills, by the force at Suddia; but the Duffa, instead of repenting of his atrocious act, and retiring to his home to await the consequences, commenced playing the despot in another quarter, threatening every one with his vengeance who acknowledged British protection, and even beheaded some who refused to conform to his will. A feud has, for a long time, existed between the Bisa and the Duffa Gaums, and the inroad lately made by the latter, admits of some palliation, as it avenged a similar one formerly made by the Bisa Gaum.

7. Caste. Rude as is the state of society amongst the Singphos, they are not without the distinction of caste; but are divided into Thengais, Myyoungs, Lubrungs, and Mirups.

8. Religion. They have no religion properly their own, but have patched up a creed from amongst the superstitions of all their neighbours, and decorated their ruder temples with ruder idols of all religions.

9. Language. The Singphos are not a branch of the Shan tribes: tradition traces their origin to the confines of China or Thibet: the language is entirely different from that of the Shans, and is unwritten.

10. Marriages.

Poligamy is patronised, and every man keeps as many wives as he chooses, free women or slaves; and treats the offspring of both without partiality. Infanticide, in all its shapes, they abhor.

11. Funeral Rites.

It is the custom of the country to bury the dead. Those of the poorer classes are interred soon after death; but the Chiefs and principal individuals are sometimes not buried for years. The reason alleged for this consummation of the funeral rites is, to allow the widely scattered relations of the deceased to have time to attend, who would not fail to take deadly offence at their not being allowed an opportunity of paying reverence to the ashes of the head of their family. Not knowing the art of embalming, the body after death is removed to a distance from any habitation, till decomposition is completed. After that it is deposited in a coffin, and conveyed to the house of the deceased Chief, where it lies in state, surrounded with all the insignia the illustrious individual enjoyed when alive. When all the relatives have assembled, or communicated their not being able to attend, the coffin is committed to the earth, and a mound of clay, surrounded with a curious trellis-work of bambus, is raised to his memory. If the person has died a violent death, a buffalo is sacrificed as a propitiation to their deities, and the head is fixed to a cross, and placed near the grave; but, if he has died in the course of nature, no sacrifice is considered necessary.

12. Inheritance.

According to the law of inheritance, the patrimony is divided between the eldest and the

XIV. HILL TRIBES. youngest sons; while any children that may intervene, are left to push their own fortunes as they best can. The eldest son succeeds to the title and the estate, while the younger carrying away all the personal and moveable property, goes in quest of a settlement for himself.

13. Intercourse with Burmese Singphos. The Singphos of Assam are separated from the Singphos subservient to the Burmese, by the Patkoi chain of mountains; and though these two races are entirely unconnected with one another and independent, yet a constant friendly intercourse is maintained between them. The Burmese Singphos occupy a very extensive tract of country on both sides of the Irrawaddi, from the Patkoi mountains eastward to the borders of China.

SECTION VIII.—MUAMARIAS OR MATTUCKS.

1, *Extent.* 2, *Devastated Assam.* 3, *Rajah.* 4, *Doubtful Fidelity.* 5, *Capital.*

1. Extent. The country of this tribe is bounded on the north by the Brahmaputra, on the south by the Buri Dihing, on the east by a line drawn south from the mouth of the Kunili nullah to the Buri

2. Devastated Assam. Dihing, and on the west by a line drawn from the mouth of the river Diburu to the Buri Dihing. About 1793 these people rose in arms against the reigning Rajah Gourinath Sing, and after many bloody engagements with the Royal troops, at last succeeded in driving him from his throne and kingdom, and in appointing a successor of their own choice. During the period

of their ascendancy, they committed the most dreadful ravages upon the country, and the original inhabitants; great portions of it were deserted, and even till this day, it has never regained any thing near its former prosperity. But these lawless plunderers were not allowed long to enjoy the fruits of their conquests; they were speedily driven from the capital by 1,000 *Sipahis* under Captain Welsh, and retreated to the district which they now inherit. XIV. HILL TRIBES.

The head of this still powerful clan is known by the name of the Mattuck Rajah, or more commonly, by that of the Bura Senaputti, (Great General.) During the Burmese War, he maintained his independence; but on our taking Rungpore, he claimed our protection, and has since manifested his sincerity, by a zealous endeavour to render every assistance in his power in the advancement of our plans. 3. Rajah.

The Bura Senaputti, with all his affability and apparent deference to our authority, is by some considered not entitled to perfect and unlimited confidence. Situated between two powerful States, the British and the Burmah, his policy seems to be to maintain good terms with both; and, in the event of another Burmese invasion, it is to be feared he would preserve neutrality, till he saw how the scale was likely to turn, and then join the stronger party. 4. Doubtful Fidelity.

The greater part of the country allotted to the Mattucks is a desert waste, and only the banks of the river Diburu are inhabited. The capital 5. Capital.

XIV. HILL TRIBES. is Rungagora. The State is allowed about three hundred musquets and ammunition according to treaty, and supplies a large contingent. They profess the Hindoo religion; but act so little in accordance with its tenets, that enlightened Brahmins scarcely acknowledge them.

SECTION IX.—NAGAS.

1, *Numerous Tribes.* 2, *Dreaded by Neighbours.* 3, *Dress.*

1. Numerous Tribes. The next border tribes met with in proceeding westward are the Nagas; these tribes are very numerous, and may amount to thirty or forty, and are scattered along the whole mountain ridge between the Sylhet plains and Assam. There is very little unanimity amongst them; they are constantly at war amongst themselves, and each village is a sort of hill fort, either made so by art or fortified by nature.

2. Dreaded by Neighbours. They are the wildest and most barbarous of all the hill tribes, and looked upon with dread and horror by the neighbours of the plains, who consider them as ruthless robbers and murderers. Many of these hordes are located in Cachar and Munnipore, and are tributary to these States.

3. Dress. The Nagas go literally naked in their hills. They have however some singular idea of modesty, which consists of having a fold of the preputium drawn through a small ivory ring, and worn in that predicament. They would think it highly indecorous to appear in female society without this ornament. These rings are

sold in the bazars of Munnipore, all of which are kept by women; and these ladies think no more about the matter in fitting a handsome Naga with this inexpressible, than they would his great toe with a ring. XIV. HILL TRIBES.

Section X.—Munnipore.

1, *Extent.* 2, *Valley.* 3, *Capitals.* 4, *Wars.* 5, *People.* 6, *Climate.*

Munnipore is divided from the Burmese empire on the east by the river Kyan-duang or Ningti, from Assam on the north by an imaginary line running east from the little river Dugang, and is bounded on the west and south by Cachar. The valley of Munnipore is not more than twelve miles in diameter, it is a perfect amphitheatre, and though elevated two or three thousand feet above the sea, is bounded by a chain of mountains, some of which are ten thousand feet high. This beautiful valley was formerly very populous and well cultivated, but it is now in a great measure left to nature, and overgrown with jungle and marshy swamps. 1. Extent. 2. Valley.

The ancient capital is now only known by ruined pagodas, clumps of large trees or mounds and ditches. Chundrapore is now the capital. 3. Capital.

In 1774 A. D. Munnipore was conquered and plundered by the Burmese, and the reigning Rajah fled for safety to Cachar. In 1806 or 1810 (the former is probably the most correct date), the kingdom devolved upon Charjit Sing, who cleared his way to the throne by the murder of two of his elder brothers, while his two 4. Wars.

XIV. HILL TRIBES. younger brothers Marjit Sing and Gumbeer Sing, who appear to have shared in the fratricide, fled for security, the former to Ava and the latter to Cachar. Marjit, having obtained the assistance of the Burmese, returning to Munnipore, drove his brother Charjit from the kingdom, and was placed on the throne on condition of paying tribute to the Burmese. In 1819, Marjit, on refusing to attend upon the King of Ava as his liege lord, was dethroned, and retiring upon Cachar with 5,000 followers, attacked Govind Chunder, the Rajah of that country, and placed himself on his throne; Govind Chunder having been betrayed by Gumbeer Sing, who commanded a small force in his service. A sort of fraternal war was for some time carried on between the brothers for the sovereignty of Cachar, when, in 1823, our Government interfered, Govind Chunder was restored to his throne, and the Munnipore brothers pensioned. In 1825 the Burmese were driven from Munnipore, and Gumbeer Sing was restored to the throne of his ancestors; Gumbeer Sing died in 1834, and was succeeded by his son Kirta Sing, a minor, the present Rajah.

5. Force. In 1832 the standing force amounted to 300 infantry, 160 cavalry and 100 artillery-men. These men get no pay, but grants of land are allowed them exempt from taxation. They are stationed in small detachments throughout the province, and when they are called into the field the crops are left to the women and children.

6. People. The Munnipooris are smart soldiers and expert horsemen; they have a large share of military

courage, and have more genius for war than most of their neighbours. They have broad Tartar features, though they profess to be Rajpoots; the women are coarse and masculine, and perform all the merchandise of the bazar. XIV. HILL TRIBES.

7. Climate. The climate of Munnipore is very different from what from its latitude might be expected; severe frosts prevail in winter, and the climate is cool and refreshing even in the hottest season of the year. Munnipore is drained by the Ningti river that falls into the Irrawaddi, and may be closely approached by conveyance on that stream. In this way the Burmese were wont to invade it. There are no carriage roads between Munnipore and Assam, but the natives have certain footpaths by which it is just possible to perform the journey.

SECTION XI.—CACHARIS.

1, *Extent*. 2, *Wars*. 3, *Royal Race extinct*. 4, *People*.

1. Extent. Cachar is bounded on the north by Assam, on the east by Munnipore, on the south by Sylhet, and on the west by Jyntea, and originally might contain an area of 9000 square miles. The ancient name of Cachar was Hairumbo, and Grobarge was the capital; the modern capital is Cospore. The river Barak is the principal line of communication on the south, the intercourse with Assam is maintained by the route already mentioned.

XIV. HILL TRIBES.

2. Wars.

In 1774 Cachar was conquered by the Burmese and made tributary, and as a ratification of the treaty the Rajah was obliged to present to the King of Ava a virgin of the royal blood, together with a tree with the soil of the country adhering to its roots. I have already observed the usurpation of Cachar by the two brothers of Munnipore, and the settlement in favor of the deposed Rajah Govind Chunder. Unfortunately, he was not long allowed to enjoy the dignity, for, on the 24th of April, 1830, he was murdered by his own soldiers at the supposed instigation of Gumbeer Sing, Rajah of Munnipore. These soldiers were Munniporis.

3. Royal Race Extinct.

The royal race of Cachar is now quite extinct. A great portion of the country is under British rule, the only remnant is now in the hands of a Hill Chief Tuliram, a soldier of fortune, and no relation to the reigning family.

4. People.

The country of Cachar is now in a great measure deserted; large colonies have settled themselves in Assam: they are a quiet industrious agricultural people, and their services are in great request. According to some accounts the Cacharis were the aborigines of Assam, and retired to Cachar on the invasion of the Ahoms. The Cacharis profess to be Hindoos, but they pay almost no regard to caste; they live freely and fully on animal food and drink as much spirits as they can afford

Section XII.—Kassyas.

1, Fierce Race of Men. 2, Massacre of Lieutenants Beddingfield and Burlton. 3, Habits. 4, Weather.

The Kassyas, the most westward but one of the southern tribes, inhabit one continued tract of country from the plains of Sylhet to Gohatti, well known by the Kassya hills, and the Sanatarium of Chirra Poonji. The Kassyas are ruled by a number of petty Rajahs, all on pretty good terms, and forming a sort of republic. They are a powerful athletic race of men, rather above the middle size than below it, with a manliness of gait and nobleness of demeanour peculiarly their own. They are proud of their mountains, and look down with contempt upon the degenerate race of the plains; jealous of their honour, warlike and brave in action, and have a regard for their pledged word, and an aversion to falsehood, little to be expected from them. I have observed the mode the Kassyas use in carrying burdens, and of their having no aversion to take up an invalid upon a chair and trudge along with their load.

1. Fierce Race of men.

An anecdote is told of a kranny on duty on the hills, once obliging a Kassya of rank, his prisoner, to give him a ride, when the Chieftain avenged the insult by throwing himself, chair, kranny and all over a precipice and was dashed to pieces.

2. Massacre of Lieuts. Beddingfield and Burlton.

I wish I could say that treachery formed no constituent in their moral character, but the

XIV. HILL TRIBES. indiscriminate and unprovoked massacre of Lieutenants Beddingfield and Burlton, and nearly their whole party stands recorded against them. These two Officers, on a treaty being concluded for a free passage across the hills, and the establishment of a sanatarium within their country, were recruiting their broken health at Nunklow, when they were suddenly beleaguered; and though they defended themselves for some days with their fowling pieces, were eventually cut to pieces. To revenge these murders active operations were immediately put in force against them. Mr. Scott, the Commissioner, was several times closely beset, and the lives of all his followers were in imminent danger; Doctor Beadon was shot by an arrow that penetrated through the nose to the brain, and he died in excruciating agony; and, for some years after, the passage over the hills could only be effected by an armed guard. However, things are at the present day very much altered, a private individual may now travel across without danger or alarm, and the Sanatarium of Chirra Poonji now abolished has still the credit of having civilized the Kassyas, and thrown open that very interesting country, which without its institution would have remained unknown.

3. Habits. The habits of the Kassyas are idle and independent, and their mode of living pastoral rather than agricultural; their houses are large and commodious, their cattle numerous, fat, and productive, and their pastures rich and abundant. Oranges, limes, cinnamon and several other fruits and spices are indigenous, the potatoe

is now extensively cultivated, and large quantities of the finest quality are transported to the plains for sale.

4. Weather.

The highest point in the Kassya hills is believed to be Moplong, its elevation is about 6,000 feet, hoar frost is common in winter, and the thermometer does not rise above 70 or 75 in the hottest weather. The climate is moist, rough and boisterous, and probably better adapted for people in robust health than for invalids. A stormy west wind blows for a great part of the year, at a high elevation this west wind passes over Assam and restores the equilibrium of the atmosphere that would otherwise be disturbed by the prevalence of easterly winds along the course of the Brahmaputra.

SECTION XIII.—GARROWS.

1, *Dress and Dainties*. 2, *Women*. 3, *Ornaments*. 4, *Nature of Country*. 5, *Unhealthiness*.

I now come to the last of all these tribes—the Garrows, who occupy that triangular extent of mountainous country between the Kassya hills and the Brahmaputra. Like the Kassyas they too are divided into numerous petty tribes, each chief of which has his vote in the assembled council, though no one of them is independent of the others. They are equally warlike with the Kassyas, superior if possible in muscular developement and bodily strength,

XIV. HILL TRIBES.

though inferior to them in external appearance and dignity of carriage. The Kassyas are more pastoral, the Garrows more agricultural; the Kassya lives by the produce of his cattle, the Garrow by the tillage of his hills; the Kassya is content to eat the bread of idleness, the Garrow loves to live by the sweat of his brow.

1. Dress and Dainties.

The Garrows go, men, women, and children, almost literally naked, and lead a life as nearly approaching that of the savage as possible. A Garrow's greatest treasure is as many human skulls as his house can contain, his greatest cordial a pint of English brandy, and his greatest dainty a pudding made by feeding a young dog with as much rice as he can hold, and then roasting him alive till the rice is cooked, when the entire mass is served up for eating. It is a remarkable fact that the Garrows abhor milk as the greatest abomination.

2. Women.

The Garrow women are amongst the ugliest pieces of female nature; sturdy and masculine, yet as fond of ornament as the fairest of the daughters of Eve. But quantity seems to have more charms for them than quality, and they are delighted with loading themselves with rings and chains, and bells of solid brass, enough to break the neck of any lady in the country.

3. Ornaments.

From ten to fifteen or more brass rings, as thick as a goose quill, and three or four inches in diameter, hang in the lobe of each ear; by whose weight they are stretched so as to touch the shoulder. The lobes being distended to a filiment eventually give way, and this is reckoned the consummation of all ornaments put together. It entitles the possessor to the envy of her own sex and the admiration of the others, and the lady moves with her torn ear, in the circle of her equals, with acknowledged superiority. One might suppose that the load in the ears might plead in apology for the neck's being free; but it also is cased in a mass of chains, proof against the hatchet of the executioner.

4. Nature of Country.

The country of the Garrows is one continued mass of hills almost without any level land, yet it is well cultivated and productive. Regular markets are held once or twice a week at convenient places along the borders. Cotton is the principal export; and, probably, an equal sum is expended at the markets in articles for home consumption.

5. Unhealthiness.

It is very remarkable, that a country producing such a powerful race of men, should be so inimical to constitutions not inured to it. Above all jungly countries in India, that of the Garrows is, perhaps, the most fatal for a European to visit. Few, or probably none, have ever penetrated one day's journey into the interior, and escaped without a severe fever; and three-fourths of those, who have done so, have fallen victims to its baneful climate.

XIV.
HILL TRIBES.

Section XIV.

Rabbas, Lalungs, Chooteas, and Mikirs.

Besides the tribes on the south of Assam already enumerated, there are several others, which have no very fixed habitations: these are, the Rabbas, Lalungs, Chooteas, and Mikirs. Neither of them are numerous enough to have any Government of their own, and they attach themselves sometimes to one State and sometimes to another, as it suits their taste or convenience.

FINIS.